Alexander Balloch Grosart, Thomas Fuller

The Poems and Translations in Verse

Including fifty-nine hitherto unpublished epigrams of Thomas Fuller, D. D.

Alexander Balloch Grosart, Thomas Fuller

The Poems and Translations in Verse
Including fifty-nine hitherto unpublished epigrams of Thomas Fuller, D. D.

ISBN/EAN: 9783337006303

Printed in Europe, USA, Canada, Australia, Japan

Cover: Foto ©Thomas Meinert / pixelio.de

More available books at **www.hansebooks.com**

THE

POEMS

AND

TRANSLATIONS IN VERSE:

(INCLUDING

FIFTY-NINE HITHERTO UNPUBLISHED EPIGRAMS)

OF

THOMAS FULLER D.D.

AND

HIS MUCH-WISHED FORM OF PRAYER;

FOR THE FIRST TIME

COLLECTED AND EDITED

WITH

Introduction and Notes

BY THE

REV. ALEXANDER B. GROSART,

LIVERPOOL.

PRINTED FOR PRIVATE CIRCULATION.

1868.

INTRODUCTION.

I SUSPECT that the first impression of those who hear of the present little volume or who take it up, will be that it is some such literary *quiz* as Sir WALTER SCOTT half-thought of perpetrating in relation to DAVID HUME. A short quotation from his genial letter will explain:—'We visited Corby Castle on our return to Scotland,' he writes to Morritt, 'which remains in point of situation as beautiful as when its walks were celebrated by David Hume, in the only rhymes he was ever know to be guilty of. Here they are, from a pane of glass in an inn at Carlisle—

> Here chickens in eggs for breakfast sprawl,
> Here godless boys God's glories squall,
> Here Scotchmen's heads do guard the wall,
> But Corby's walks atone for all.'

Then playfully, 'Would it not be a good quiz to advertise the *Poetical Works of David Hume*, with notes, critical, historical, and so forth—with an historical inquiry into the use of eggs for breakfast, a physical discussion on the causes of

their being addled, a history of the English
Church music and of the choir of Carlisle in
particular ; a full account of the affair of 1745,
with the trials, last speeches and so forth, of the
poor *plaids* who were strapped up at Carlisle ;
and lastly, a full and particular description of
Corby, with the genealogy of every family who
ever possessed it ? I think even without more
than the usual *waste* of margin, the Poems of
David would make a decent twelve shilling
touch. I shall think about it when I have
exhausted mine own century of inventions.'[1]
Even students of FULLER I find have never so
much as seen his longest 'Divine Poem,' are
unfamiliar with his 'Panegyrick,' and have over-
looked his lesser things. So that unless I much
mistake this volume of 'Poems and Translations'
bearing his sunny name will come as a surprise
—a pleasant surprise surely—to not a few of his
lovers. But they will not be 'bamboozled' (if
the slang word be allowable) with any such
'Notes' and 'Inquiries' as loveable SIR WALTER
jocosely designed for HUME's quatrain.

I had resolved to edit and print a limited
private edition of 'David's Hainous Sinne, Heartie
Repentance, Heavie Punishment,' and the 'Pane-

---

[1] Life by Lockhart c. xxxv.

gyrick,' as on talking with fellow-reverers of
FULLER, I discovered that not one in a score had
once met with them, while all were wishful to
have them if only they might be purchased under
Bibliomania-price. My own copy of the former
had cost me £5, 5s., and the latter £2, 2s.;[1]
and inquiry soon satisfied that in the book-
market they were deemed cheap at these (com-
paratively) high prices, *e.g.* in the British
Museum copy which is bound in saffron morocco,
but cropped mended and soiled, there is a memo-
randum that it had sold for £17 at Brand's Sale
(whose book-plate is on it); and for the 'Panegyrick'—which is in virgin state, uncut edges—I
was soon offered £3, 3s. So that—independent
of intrinsic worth and interest—if these could be
faithfully and worthily reproduced for fewer pence
than the pounds they readily fetch in the original
editions, I thought a little literary service should
be rendered thereby. But on proceeding to carry
this out it soon appeared that more was demanded.

---

[1] A copy of David's Hainous Sinne, etc., was recently
on sale by Mr Joseph Lilly (a bookseller of the fine old
stamp), Covent Garden, London, thus described, 'a Poem,
small octavo, calf extra, gilt edges, the last leaf containing
the concluding (only) verses reprinted, £5, 5s.' I believe
it was snapped up instantly. Bindley's copy brought
£5, 15s. 6d. Hibbert's, which was the same copy, £6, 6s.

For on turning to my marked copies of the
'Worthies,' 'Church-History,' 'Pisgah-Sight:' in
short to Fuller's complete Works, I came on
many 'Verses'—mainly translations from the
Latin—having, occasionally at least, the salt of
wit, the dainty fancies, the inimitable word-play
and alliteration, the brilliant conceits—as of
ancient torcs of gold—the kindly humour, the
soft delicate pitifulness, of this most loveable of
England's Worthies. [I don't—as usual—call
him 'dear *old* Fuller:' for alas! he died aged
only 53]. All this being so, I concluded to give
the *whole* of his Poems and Verse-Translations.
Still further: My attention having been oblig-
ingly called by Mr W. C. Hazlitt to his communication to Notes and Queries (3d Series vii.
pp. 352, 353), concerning a volume formerly
belonging to him, wherein were written in a
contemporary hand a large number of Epigrams
by 'Mr Tho. Fuller,' inquiries were set on foot
to discover its present possessor. By the kind
zeal of Mr F. S. Ellis, Bookseller, 33 King
Street, Covent Garden, London, I speedily re-
covered the precious little book, and obtained
unreserved permission to use whatever I might
wish in it. The Epigrams authenticate themselves: many being truly Fullerian. I congratu-
late myself on my rare good fortune in having it

in my power to add this treasure-trove to my collection. I beg to return right hearty thanks to its owner (H. H. Gibbs Esq., London), for his ready liberality that enables me to do this.

Thus the present volume—as its title-page bears—not only furnishes Fuller's larger Poems, but 'for the first time' brings together the minor ' Verses ' scattered up and down his numerous prose writings, and no fewer than fifty-nine hitherto unpublished Epigrams by him.

Regarding 'the Poems and Translations' intrinsically, I prefix—in its place—the Criteism of his longest poem by OLDYS. But he has missed its biographic interest and its most characteristic turns and touches. Biographically it is to be remembered that as 'David's Hainous Sinne,' etc. was published in 1631 it was probably composed when he was little out of his ' teens.'—So that his first known production confirms Charles Lamb's penetrative insight in his winsome words on his genius: 'The writings of Fuller are usually designated by the title of quaint and with sufficient reason : *for such was his natural bias* to conceits, that I doubt not, upon most occasions, *it would have been going out of his way* to have expressed himself out of them.' In his earliest as in his last book is the same ' Roman hand,' the same inevitableness, naturalness and spontaneity of 'quaint' thought and wording. I cull a few examples of word-play from 'David's Hainous Sinne :' and sure I am that no one familiar with FULLER will fail to detect in them the very *essentia* of his after-style. Thus he puts poor Uriah's eager obedience in carrying the king's false and fatal ' Letter,'—

> On his journey past
> With speed, who needed not to make such hast
> Whose death had he gone slow did come too fast.
>
> [I. st. 33.]

Again, wisely as well as wittily :

> Where
> *Kings bid and God forbids,* we must forbeare
> [*Ibid.* st. 44.]

And of Uriah finely—

> Thus of his friends betray'd by subtill traine :
> Assaulted of his foes with might and maine
> *He lost his life, not conquerèd but slain*
> [*Ibid.* st. 46.]

So of the 'infant newly borne, now neare to dye' very tenderly—

> See with what silent signes and sighes full faine
> Poore heart it would expresse where lies the paine
> Complaining that it knowes not to complaine
> [III. st. 3.]

Again—

> His tongue did never lye that cannot speke.
> [*Ibid.* st. 5.]

Then follows this dainty metaphor—

> As when a tender rose begins to blow
> Yet scarce unswadled is, some wanton maide
> Pleas'd with the smell, allured with the show
> Will not reprive it till it hath display'd
> The folded leaves: but to her brest applies
> Th' abortive budd, where coffinèd it lyes
> *Losing the blushing dye before it dies.* [*Ibid.* st. 7.]

Here is a genuinely FULLERIAN and later GEORGE CRABBE-ian alliteration—on 'the poor larke imprison'd in the cage of a kite's claws' vainly pleading for escape

> On her that pray'd so long, doth prey at last.
> [*Ibid.* st. 14.][1]

Again: of Absalom's mock-condescension—

> He steales their hearts by taking of their hands.
> [*Ibid.* st. 25.]

Incisively too

> A saint dissembled is a double devile. [*Ibid.* st. 28.]
> Asse, that for wit his rider did exceed. [*Ibid.* st. 34.]

Then, more fully and with still more characteristic touches:

---

[1] We have many like lines *e.g.* of the 'asse' whereon Absalom rode, set free
> Now rid of him that rid on her before. [III. st. 45.]
So—
> A fruitfull wildernesse of fruitlesse weeds. [*Ibid.* st. 48.]
> Seldome things done speedily doe speed. [*Ibid.* st. 53.]
> Losing their gettings, gaining what they lost.
> [*Ibid.* st. 68.]

> A chayne of hempe he to his necke made fast
> By tying of which knot he did untye
> The knot of soule and body, and at last
> Stopping the passage of his breath, thereby
>> A passage for his soule wide opened hee :
>> Thus traytors rather than they should goe free
>> Themselves the hangman of themselves will bee.
>>>> [*Ibid.* st. 37.]

Again :

> My sonne! whose body had of grace the fill
> My sonne! whose soule was so devoid of grace.
>>>> [*Ibid.* st. 50.]

Further : This 'Divine poem' is of biographic interest and value in that it reveals FULLER's Calvinism at the time (at least)—on two leading 'doctrines' *e.g.* Predestination or Election.

> . . Soone with a word the Lord appeas'd this strife
> Injoyning silence till he did vnfold
> That precious volume cald the Booke of Life
> Which He the Printer priviledg'd of old
>> Containing those He freely did imbrace :
>> Nor ever would I wish an higher grace
>> Than in this Booke to hae the lowest place.
>
> Within this Booke he sought for David's name
> Which having found He proffered to blot
> (And David surely well deserv'd the same
> That did his nature so with sinne bespot)
>> Though none are blotted out but such as never
>> Were written in ; nothing God's love can sever ;
>> Once written there are written there for ever.
>>>> [II. st. 5, 6.]

Similarly on Original Sin :—

> But ah! this infant's guilt from him proceeds
> That knew the least when most he sought to know:
> Who most was nak't when cloathed in his weeds
> Best cloathed then when naked he did goe:
>> In vayne the wit of wisest men doth strive
>> To cut off this intayle, that doth derive
>> Death unto all when first they are alive.
>
> [III. st. 6.]

It is only due to our Worthy to add his ' charitable ' stanza on the absence of the rite of baptism :

> So this babe's life, newly begun, did end
> Which sure receiv'd the substance though not sign'd
> With grace's seale: God freely doth attend
> His ordinance, but will not be confin'd
>> Thereto when 'tis not neglected nor despis'd
>> They that want water are by fire baptiz'd
>> Those sanctify'd that ne're were circumcis'd.
>
> [III. st. 8.]

Besides these theological opinions we have in this Poem—and elsewhere—unmistakeable utterances on kindred matters. I select these four—prefixing headings—

1. *Drunkenness :*

> My prayers for friends prosperity and wealth
> Shall ne're be wanting: but if I refuse
> To hurt myself by drinking others' health
> Oh let ingenious natures mee excuse:
>> If men bad manners this esteeme, then I
>> Desire to be esteem'd unmannerly
>> That to live well will suffer wine to dye.
>
> [I. st. 27.]

2. *Preaching :*

Goe fond affectors of a flanting straine
Whose sermons strike at sinnes with slenting blowes!
Give me the man that's powerfull and plaine
The monster Vice vnmasked to expose :
   Such preachers doe the soule and marrow part
   And cause the guilty conscience to smart
   Such pleaso no itching eares but peirce tho heart.

                                  [II. st. 22.]

3. *Female-humility :*

Ah! happy age when ladies learn't to bake
And when kings daughters knew to knead a cake.
Rebecka was esteem'd of comely hew
Yet not so nice her comelinesse to keepe
But that shee water for tho cammells drew:
Rachell was faire, yet fedd her father's shoepe
   But now for to supply Rebecka's place
   Or doe as Rachell did is counted base:
   Our dainty dames would take it in disgrace.[1]

                             [III. st. 11, 12.]

---

[1] This reminds me of an anecdote of a quaint old Scotch 'minister' of the last century (Mr Comrie of Pennicuik). His Congregation had been engaged in making a pecuniary effort to pay off debt on the Church by a kind of anticipation of what are now called Bazaars. It did not prove a success ; and mainly through the lack of zeal of tho ladies. Chagrined, Mr Comrie in a speech afterwards, looking the gay-dressed fair ones full in the face remarked dryly, ' The leddies noo-a-days pit me in mind o' tho Lilies [All attention expecting a compliment]—*they toil not neither do they spin.*'

4. *False-friendship:*

Before such kisses come vpon my face
Oh! let the deadly scorpion me sting
Yea rather than such armes should me imbrace
Let curling snakes about my body cling:
   Than such faire words I'de rather the fowle
   Vntuned schreeching of the dolefull owle
Or heare the direfull mountaine-wolfe to howle.
                    [*Ibid.* st. 26.]

I must leave the reader to dig for like *nuggets.* Preceded by GEORGE PEELE in his 'Love of King David and Fair Bet'sabe with the Tragedie of Absalom' (1599) and coming into comparison with the 'Davideis; a heroical poem on the troubles of David,' of ABRAHAM COWLEY —his contemporary and fellow-student at Cambridge—Fuller's first Poem loses nothing beside them.

The 'Panegyrick' has happy lines: and was the genuine utterance of our large-hearted Worthy's loyalty to his ideal of monarchy. Hence the transfiguration of Charles the Second. Historically it is valuable as an evidence of the glowing hopes that centred in the 'merry monarch.' The actual 'Life' Fuller did not witness. He was 'gone' before the brightness of the exile-years paled into foulest Night. High-pitched as is his praise it is low compared with innumerable contemporary 'Welcomes' still preserved in the British Museum and elsewhere.[1]

The Translation-verses I have already characterized: though truth to tell many of them only two faithfully answer his own apologetic description, 'Yet because some love poetry, either very good or very bad, that if they cannot learn from it, they may laugh at it, they are here inserted.'[2] Others are in daintiness of wording and quaintness of their turns as the Songs of Shakespere and Jonson to their Plays. The 'Flowers' must lose in their transplantation (or cutting) even with the words as so much living

---

[1] One of the most astounding of these productions is the following ΚΑΡΟΛΟΥ τρεσμεγιστου Ἐπιφανια: The Most Gloriovs Star or Celestial Constellation of the Pleiades or Charles Waine. Appearing and shining most brightly in a *Miraculous* manner in the Face of the Sun at Noon day at the Nativity of our Sacred Soveraign King *Charles* 2. Presaging his Majesties *Exaltation* to future Honour and Greatness, Transcending not only the most potent Christian Prince, *in Europe*, but by Divine Designment ordained to be the most *Mighty Monarch* in the *Vniverse*. Never any Starre having appeared before at the birth of any (the *Highest humane Hero*) except our Saviour. Behold a King shall reign in righteousness. Psal. 32. 1. By Edw. Mathew of the Middle *Temple* Esq. London, Printed for the use and benefit of William Byron, Gent. 1662 [12°]—Title-page— Ep: Dedy pp. 12—Treatise pp. 156—Two engravings adorn (!) the volume.

[2] 'Worthies' [London].

earth—*Fuller's* earth, Fuller himself would have said—attached : ay, were they put into 'Pots' such as Keats' 'basil' grew in. Still I have given as much of the context in which the 'Verses' occur as to impart interest.

I do not at all claim poetic genius for 'rare' THOMAS FULLER, or for independent poetic fame. But everything that serves to furnish insight into the whole nature of a great man has its own use and worth. It *is* noticeable that while he did not follow up his 'David's Hainous Sinne,' etc., with other poems of like-length and kin, he yet kept singing unto the end. There must have been a string that vibrated to the subtle 'bréath' when the music—and words to it—was so inevitable and irrepressible. Biographers and critics have failed as it seems to us, to recognise this element in the large, rich, most winsome nature of our Worthy.

I scrupulously adhere to the original text throughout, retaining FULLER's own orthography:[1]

---

[1] I must ask the student, however, to keep in mind that with very few exceptions the present apostrophe of the possessive case was unemployed by Fuller and his contemporaries—*e.g.*, we read not Truth's but Truths, Romes not Rome's. I have also somewhat modified the use of capitals and italics, which are used very arbitrarily.

agreeing herein with the venerated Keble that
' in one respect especially, *i.e.* as a specimen and
monument of language, ancient books lose very
much of their value by the neglect of ancient
orthography.'[1] For popular, practical use, mo-
dernization of spelling is not only permissible,
but absolutely necessary. On the other hand,
to the circle to whom this reprint addresses itself,
faithfulness to the author is a *sine qua non.* I
have used all the care that I could command:
and I venture to hope not in vain.[2] A few
Notes explanatory of names and references, bear
my initial G. Those of Fuller himself, F. Of
course in the Translation-Verses and originals
from his prose Works the reader must turn to
the several places for further information as to
names and things introduced. It were mis-
placed annotation to enlarge on these in such a
small venture as the present.

Besides the Poems and Verse-Translations

---

[1] Keble's Hooker, Vol. I.: Preface page viii (edn. 1841,
3 vols. 8°). I have marked the noticeable words in foot-
notes.

[2] I cannot expect to be found faultless, for even so
scholarly and able an editor as Dr Nuttall in his edition of
the ' Worthies' very often errs—*e.g.,* in No. LIV. of our
extracts from the ' Worthies' he misreads 'paths for parts,'
and reduces the sweet couplet to nonsense: in No. LXIV.
for 'townsmen' reads ' townmen.'

and Epigrams as enumerated, I give as an
Appendix the 'Form of Prayer' used by Dr
Fuller. The book in which it is contained is
of the very rarest: and hence in Notes and
Queries and elsewhere this 'Form' has been
repeatedly inquired for—in vain. To the eru-
dite Librarian of Trinity College, Cambridge (W.
Aldis Wright, Esq., M.A.) I am indebted for
this addition to the Fulleriana of our volume.

I close this Introduction with some pat lines
from that finely-touched old Translator—ARTHUR
GOLDING, which I have chanced on unreferenced
in my Common Place Book :—

> Whoso doth attempt this Author's works to read
> Must bring with him a stayèd head and judgment to
> proceed ;
> For as there be most wholesome hests and precepts to
> be found
> So are there rocks and shallow shelves to run the ship
> a-ground.

ALEXANDER B. GROSART.

308 UPPER PARLIAMENT STREET,
 LIVERPOOL.

P.S.—As I send my Manuscript to the
Printers there reaches me a reprint of 'David's
Hainous Sinne, etc., tacked on to Fuller's Party-
coloured-Coat, a Comment on 1 Corinthians xi.,'
etc. The volume is edited by Mr William Nichols,

and forms one of a number of Fuller-reprints
from the house of Tegg—most welcome! But
the *modernisation* of the orthography of the Poem
is inexcusable. In no respect can it come into
competition with our volume apart from its
giving only *one* of the poetic productions of the
Author. G.

CONTENTS.

CONTENTS.

*** Owing to an oversight, the verses from the ' Profane State ' in our book are numbered XI. instead of XII., and those that follow ought to have continued XIII., XIV., XV., XVI., XVII., XVIII. Notice that † opposite verses indicate that they are original, not translated.   G.

LDYS on 'David's Hainous Sinne,' etc., from Biographia Britannica [Vol. iii. page 2050, folio.] 'The first performance of our author that has appeared to us in print, being a divine poem, very rare to be met with, and having had no description of it, the following account may not be unacceptable to the curious. It is entitled . . A critical reader of poetry might find matters of remark in it; either to commend in some agreeable descriptions, natural similies, and instructive reflections; or to censure in some few parts of the style, which were fashionable elegancies in those times: but in the whole promising that had he persevered in the study and culture of poetry, his genius might have advanced him to some considerable rank among those contemporaries who were then favorites of the Muses. His good sense and ingenuity at that age is distinguishable enough; his versification is more compact or limited, and usually flows with smoother cadence than that of some riper wits

of great name in those days. Among other
observable parts, the very proposition and in-
vocation are very comprehensive, solemn, and
regular : the persuasions of David by the Spirit
and the Flesh ; with the description of Uriah's
drunkenness, are very natural : the obsequious
offer of the Elements to destroy David upon his
transgression, and after his restitution to relieve
and cherish him, are somewhat picturesque, and
touching upon Spencer's imag[e]ry in miniature :
his comparison of those variable elements upon this
occasion, to temporising courtiers, who will fawn
upon a minister when he is restored to favour, as
fast as they flouted him in disgrace, looks to have
something in it perfectly alive ; and so does that
figure wherein we may imagine that we see
Absalom cringing with supple neck and knees
about the court, to gather up what alms and
fragments he could of popular favour and interest,
by seizing upon one man's hand to steal away
his heart, and sucking out the soul of another
with deceitful kisses ; inquiring the name of this,
the business of that, and the country of t'other,
to serve them all ! prostituting his promises and
enslaving himself to errant slaves : in whom also
we have a further glimpse of pride itself, grovel-
ling to be exalted to grandeur, and exercising all
the abject spirit of the most beggarly poor, to

worm itself into riches : or as one author reads
it—

> · Proud men are base to compass their desires ;
> They lowest crouch that highest do aspire.'[1]

But this is a picture not near so agreable as that
of plain-dealing Nathan, in his state of moderation ; the knowing and communicative, the kind
and compassionate Nathan, who being skilled in
lancing a fester'd soul, in searching and tenting
the sore, and stanching a bleeding-hearted sinner,
would heal his wounds with the sovereign balsam
of counsel, or bind up the disjointed members of
his troubled mind. He was neither oppressed
with that plenty which made him envied nor
distressed with that penury which made him
despised : his pursuits were circumscribed to his
possessions ; and as he was in no needful want,
he thought wanton need most despicable ; or
that want in sufficiency was the true mother of
contempt : so, as his desires were planted within
the most temperate situations of command, they

---

[1] A similar turn of thought occurs in his *Andronicus* when
the usurper ceremoniously kissed the feet of the young
monarch. 'The spectators variously commented on his
prodigious humility therein ; some conceiving *he meant to
build high because he began so low.*' G.

produced the sweetest fruits of content; for, as
our poet says :

'High hills are parch'd with heat or hid with snow,
And humble dales, soon drown'd, that lie too low,
Whilst happy grain on hanging hills doth grow.'[1]

Descriptions more flowery might be hither transplanted; such as are so gently strewed over
David's child in death, and others; but as his
gravity in this poem prevails over the natural
gaiety of his genius, we have chosen in this historical work to instance those few particulars which
are rather in the edifying and profitable than to
hunt after such as may run into a more pleasing
and poetical vein. At the close of this performance our author having subsided into the
characters of Queen Elizabeth, King James, and
King Charles I., and lamented the loss of the

---

[1] Campbell uses a somewhat similar figure where he
speaks of the stations of life best fitted for Tragedy :

'Even situations far depressed beneath the familiar
mediocrity of life are more picturesque and poetical than
its ordinary level. It is, certainly, on the virtues of the
middling ranks of life that the strength and comforts of
society chiefly depend, in the same manner as we look for
the harvest, not in cliffs and precipices, but on the easy
slope and uniform plain.'—*Specimens.*

This sentiment well comports with F.'s moderate life.
But he was no *neuter* 'of that lukewarm temper which
heaven and hell doth hate.'—(ANDRONICUS). G.

Duke of Brunswick, with the discords then in
Europe thro' the wars in the Netherlands, Den-
mark, etc., he very properly and piously con-
cludes that those grievances may be bewailed
by mankind but till they are reversed by Providence, they are more befitting his *prayers* than
his *pen*.'

I. DAVID'S HAINOUS SINNE.

NOTE.

The original title-page of this 'Divine Poem' will be found below.* The collation is as follows: Title-page —Dedication 1 page—Poem pp. 73—[12º.]—G.

*   HAINOVS SINNE.

David's   HEARTIE Repentance.

        HEAVIE Punishment.

Exodus 35. 23.

And every man, with whom was found ——— Goates haire, and red skins of Rammes, and Badgers skins. brought them [to the building of the Tabernacle].

Ad Zoilum.

Thy Laics thou vtt'rest not, yet carpest mine
Carpe mine no longer, or else vtter thine.

By Thomas Fvller, Master of Arts of Sidnye
Colledge in Cambridge.

London,
Printed by *Tho. Cotes*, for *Iohn Bellamie*. dwelling at the three Golden Lyons in Cornehill, 1631.[1]

---

[1] It may be noted that '*Thomas Cotes*' was the printer and publisher of Shakespere's folio of 1632 (Second edition). G.

To the honorable Mr Edward, Mr William,
and Mr Christopher Montagu, sonnes to the
Right honourable Edward Lord Montagu of
Boughton.[1]

FAIRE branches of a stock as faire
Each a sonne and each an heire:
Two Joseph-like from sire so sage,
Sprung in autumne of his age;
But a Benjamin the other
Gain'd with losing of his mother.
This fruit of some spare hours I spent
To your Honours I present.

A king I for my subject have
And noble patrons well may crave;
Things tripartite are fit for three,
With youths, things youthful best agree;
Take them therefore in good part
Of him that ever prayeth in heart
That as in height ye waxe apace,
Your souls may higher grow in grace.

[1] Full information concerning this historic family,
and these 'youths' in particular, will be found in 'Court
and Society from Elizabeth to Anne. Edited from the
Papers of Kimbolton by the Duke of Manchester,' 2 vols.
8vo. 1864. Cf: I. 266 seqq 273 seqq, et alibi. One of the
maps in 'Pisgah-Sight' is dedicated to the Montagus. G.

Whilst your father (like the greene
Eagle in his scutcheon seene :
Which with bill his age doth cast)
May longer still and longer last :
To see your vertues o're increase
Your yeares, ere he departs in peace.
Thus I my booke to make an end
To you : and you to God commend.

Your Honours in all service
Tho. Fuller.

DAVID'S HAINOUS SINNE.

1.

OW Zion's Psalmist grievously
offended
How Israel's Harper did most
foulely slide,
Yet how that Psalmist penitent, amended
And how that Harper patient did abide
Deserved chastisement (so fitly stil'd
Which wrath inflicted not but love most mild
Not for to hurt but heale a wanton child.)

2.

How one by her owne brother was defiled
And how that brother by a brother slaine ;
And how a father by his sonne exiled :
And by a subject, had a soveraigne :
How peace procured after battels fierce
As Sol at length doth sullen cloudes dispierce :
My Muse intends the subject of her verse.

3.

Great God of might whose power most soveraigne
Depends of none yet all of Thee depend,

Time cannot measure, neither place containe
Nor wit of man Thy being comprehend :
  For whil'st I thing on Three, I am confin'd
  To One, and when I One conceive in minde
  I am recal'd to Three in One combin'd

4.

Thy helpe I crave, Thy furtherance I aske
My head, my heart, my hand direct and guide,
That whil'st I vndertake this weighty taske
I from Thy written lore start not aside :
  Alas ! 'tis nothing Lord with Thee to breake
  The strong : 'tis nothing to support the weake
  To make men dumbe, to make an infant
    speake.

5.

Each one begotten by immortall seed
Becomes the pitcht feild of two deadly foes ;
Spirit and flesh, these never are agreed
With trucelesse warre each other doth oppose ;
  And though the spirit oft the flesh doth quell
  It may subdue but can it not expell
  So stoutly doth the Jebusite rebell.

6.

Now David when on Bathsheba loose eyes
He fixt, his heavenly halfe did him disswade ;

Turne, turne away thy sight from vanities
Exchange thy object, else thou wilt be made
   Vnmindfull of thy soule, her corps[1] to minde
   Made for to lose the truth, such toyes to finde,
   By looking long, made at the last, starke
      blinde.

7.

What though her face and body be most faire,
Behold, the sun her beauty doth surpass ;
His golden beames surmount[2] her yellow hayre
As far as purest cristall dyrtic glasse :
   Her skinne as is the skie not halfe so cleare
   Her curious veines for colour come not neare
   Those azure streaks that in the heavens
      appeare.

8.

There let thy hungry sight her famine feede,
Whereon it cannot surfet with excesse :
Whil'st tongue, heart, harp are tuned vp with
      speed,
The grand-contrivers glory to expresse :
   Framing with words to rayse his mighty name
   That with a mighty word did rayse this frame,
   And by his providence preserves the same.

---

[1] The latin 'corpus' body, not necessarily life-less. G.
[2] Surpass *e.g.* Shakespere 1 Henry VI. v. 3. and Love's
Labour Lost v. 2. G.

9.

But let no lustfull thoughts lodge in thy minde,
Before that they be borne, they must be kill'd,
Or else the man is cruell that is kinde
To spare the foes wherewith his soule is spill'd :
  And if a wanton motion may request,
  Leave for to lodge a limbe th' incroaching
    guest
  Will soone command roome to receive the
    rest.

10.

Looke towards the mid-day sun, and thou shalt
    see
A little tower[1] o're topps of hills to peepe ;
That is the birth place of thy pedygree :
Full oft there hast thou fed thy father's sheepe,
  And kept his flockes vpon the flowry plaine :
  But now the sheepe-hook of a country swaine
  Is turn'd the scepter of a soveraigne.

11.

God made thee great, oh doe not Him disgrace
And by His weighty statutes lightly set :

---

[1] The tower of Eder nigh Bethlehem 7 miles from Jerusalem. F.

Hee honour'd thee, oh doe not Him debase;
Hee thee remembred, doe not Him forget :
  Why should fat[1] Jeshurun so wanton grow
  As at his maister's head his heeles to throw?
  Maister: that all his feeding did bestow.

12.

Behold high cedars in the valley set
They in thy eyes like little shrubbs doe show,
Whil'st little shrubbs vpon mount Oliuet
Seeme lofty cedars : men whose states are low
  Their sinnes are not so obvious to sense :
  In princes, persons of great eminence
  A smaller fault doth seeme a great offence.

13.   .

But grant, no man thy wickednes espies
Surely the Searcher of the reines doth marke
Even infant lust? can figg-leaves bleare his
  eyes?
Or can thy shame bee shrowded in the darke?
  Darknes shall then be turned into light
  Yea darknes is no darknes, in His sight
  But seeme the same to Him both day and
  night.

---

[1] Deut. xxxii. 15.   F.

14.

The Spirit had resolved more to speake
But her halfe-spoken words the Flesh confounds:
Nor wonder is it, she so vs'd to breake
God's lawes, not passing for to passe their bounds
Against man's rules of manners should offend
Which was impatient longer to attend
Began before her rivall made an end.

15.

If euer nature lavishly did throw
Her gifts on one which might haue served more
Yet make them comely : if shee e're did show
The prime, and pride, and plenty of her store.
Loe, there's the forme wherein she hath
exprest
Her utmost power, and done the very best
Her maister-peece surpassing all the rest.

16.

What if those carelesse tresses were attired?
Sure then her face for comelines transcends :
What now seemes lovely then would be admired,
If art might but begin where nature ends.
Alas! ten thousand pitties 'tis indeed
That princes on so common fare should feed
Whilst common men on princely meat exceed.

17.

Alwayes the same doth glut the appetite
But pleased is our palate with exchange ;
Variety of dishes doth delight :
Then give thy loose affections leave to range.
  Forbidden things are best, and when we eate
  What we have slily gotten by deceit :
  Those morsels onely make the daynty meate.

18.

But oh reserve thy selfe, my maiden muse
For a more modest subject, and forbeare
To tune such wanton toyes as may abuse
And give distaste vnto a virgin's eare :
  Such rotten reasons first from hell did flow
  And thither, let the same in silence goe,
  Best knowne of them that did them never know.

19.

Thus hee that conquer'd men and beast most
    cruell
(Whose greedy pawes with fellon goods were
    found)
Answer'd Goliath's challenge in a duell
And lay'd the giant groveling on the ground :
  He that of Philistines two hundred slue
  No whit appalled at their grisly hue
  Him one frayle woman's beauty did subdue.

20.

Man is a shippe, affections the sayle
The world the sea, our sinnes the rocks and
   shelves,
God is the pylot, if He please to fayle
And leave the stearing of us to ourselves
   Against the rugged rocks wee run amaine
   Or else the winding shelves doe us detaine
   Till God the Palinure returns againe.

21.

Yet David bold to sinne, did fear the shame :
He shunn'd the sheath that ran upon the knife :
With a fine fetch[1] providing for his fame
He fetcheth home Vriah to his wife :
   So under his chaste love to cloake his owne
   Vnlawful lust to fault most carelesse growne,
   Most carefull that his fault should not be
   knowne.

22.

But in their plots God doth befoole the wise
By wayes that none can trace, all must admire :
Short of his house that night Vriah lyes,
And David so came short of his desire :
   The man a nearer lodging place did use

---

[1] Expedient.   G.

(Which made the king on further plots to
   muse)
And sent home, home to goe, did thus refuse.

23.

The pilgrime arke doth sojourne in a tent :
In open fields Joab my lord doth lye,
And all the souldiers of his regiment
Have earth their beds, the heaven their canopy :
   Where bitter blasts of stormy winds are rife.
   Shall I goe feast, drink, dally with my wife?
   Not, as I live, and by your lordship's life.

24.

Then by his servants David did conspire
Uriah's lust so dull, with wine to edge :
(Venus doth freeze where Bacchus yeelds no fire)
By their constraint, he condescends to pledge
   One common cup that was begun to all
   Captaines incamped nigh to Rabba wall ;
   One specially vnto the generall.

25.

Abishay next is drunke to Joab's brother
And this cupp to a second paves the way ;
That orderly doth vsher in another :
Thus wine once walking knowes not where to
   stay :

Yea such a course methodicall they take
In ordering of cupps the same did make
Vriah quite all order to forsake.

26.

His false supporters soone began to slipp
And if his faltring tongue doth chance to light
On some long word hee speedily doth clip
The traine thereof: yea his deceitfull sight
  All obiects paired doth present to him :
  As double faces ; both obscure and dim
  Seeme in a lying looking-glasse to swim.

27.

My prayers for friends prosperity, and wealth
Shall ne're be wanting, but if I refuse
To hurt myself by drinking others health
Oh let ingenious natures mee excuse :
  If men bad manners this esteeme, then I
  Desire to be esteem'd unmannerly
  That to live well will suffer wine to dye.

28.

Well did blind Homer see, for to expresse
The vice that spawnes all other, when he faines
Dame Circe an inchanting sorceresse
Whose cupps made many men foregoe their
    braines

Whilst with the witlesse asse one purely[1] doats
Others mishaped are, like lustfull goates,
Or swil-ingrossing swine, with greedy throats.

29.

Though bad yet better was Vriah left :
Not quite a beast though scarse a man; disturb'd
In minde, but not distracted nor bereft
Of witt ; though drunk yet soberly hee curb'd
   His lust; being wise though ignorant, to crosse
   The kings designes who now new thoughts
      doth tosse
   Finding his former project at a losse.

30.

The night with mourning-weeds the world becladd
When restlesse David for to mend his matter
Did make it worse : his naked sinne was bad
More monstrous being maskt ; they oft doe scatter
   The chayne that of God's lawes vnloose a linke :
   Hee swam before in sinne nigh to the brinke
   But now he meanes in midst thereof to sinke.

31.

Then for a light hee speedily did call
(Thou Darknes with his project best agree'd !)

---

[1] Prettily.   G.

For paper, pen and inke, to write withall
Though sure a poinard might have don the deed
   Better if hee in blood had dippèd it
   And on a sheet of paper what he writ
   A winding sheet far better did befit.

32.

This certs I know as sepian juice did sinke
Into his spongy paper, sabling o're
The same with various-formèd specks of inke
Which was so pure and lilly-white before :
   So spots of sinne the writers soule did staine
   Whose soylie tincture did therein remaine
   Till brinish tears had washt it out againe.

33.

Next day when Day was scarce an infant growne
Vriah (that no mischiefe did mistrust
As none hee did decerve, but by his owne
Did measure all men's dealings to bee just)
   Bearing this letter, on his journey past
   With speed, who needed not to make such hast
   Whose death had he gone slow did come too
      fast.

34.

Thus crafty maisters when they minde to beate
A carelesse boy to gather birch they send him ;

The little lad doth make the rod compleat
Thinking his maister therefore will commend
    him:
  But busily imploy'd, he little thought
  Hee made the net wherein himselfe was caught
  And must be beaten with the birch hee brought.

35.

His journey came well to the welcome end
Safe to the[1] towne of waters hee attaines
Towne which to force Joab his force did bend
(Nought is so hard but vincible by paines)
  Some with their heads did plot, some with
      their hands
  Did practise yea as ready was the band
  To serve as was the captaine to command.

36.

So busie bees, some fly abroad at large
Of flowry nectar for to fetch their fill:
Some stay at home for to receive their charge
And trustily the liquor doe distill:
  Or bottle it in waxe, whilst others strive
  Like sturdy martialls, far away to drive
  The drowsy droanes that harbour in the hive.

---

[1] Rabba. 2 Sam. xii. 27. F.

D

37.

The strong-arm'd archer from his crooked bow
Made a strait shaft with dismall newes to speed
Into the towne, which ne're return'd to show
The sender how his message did succeed :
  Yea heavie bodies mounted were on high,
  Dull stones to which dame Nature did deny
  Feete for to goe, Art made them wings to fly.

38.

Whilst in the towne one with his friend did talk
A sudden stroake did take his tongue away ;
Some had their leggs arrested as they walke
By martiall law commanding them to stay :
  Here falls a massy beame, a mighty wall
  Comes tumbling there, and many men doth
    maule
  Who were both slaine and buried by the fall.

39.

Were there not vs'd in the days of yore
Enough men-murdering engines? but our age
Witty in wickednes must make them more,
By new found plotts mens malice to inrage :
  So that fire-spitting canons to the cost
  Of Christian blood all valour have ingrost,
  Whose finding makes that many a life is
    lost.

40.

Whilst thus the well-appointed army fought
Winding in worm-like trenches neare the wall
To humble the proud towers, Vriah brought
The speaking paper to the generall
    Who when such language hee therein did
    finde
    He thought himselfe or els the King vs blinde,
    Himselfe in body or the King in minde.

41.

Then hee the letter did peruse againe
The words, the words of David could not bee
And yet the hand, for David's hand was plaine.
Hee thought it was and thought it was not hee :
    Each little line he thorowly did view
    Till at the length more credulous he grew
    And what he thought was false he found too
    true.

42.

Now Joab thy valour be display'd
Act not a midwife to a deed vnjust ;
By feare or favour be not oversway'd
To prove a pander to a prince's lust :
    Returne a humble answer back agane
    Let each word breath submission, to obtaine
    By prayers a conquest of thy soueraigne.

43.

Shew how when God and countries good requires
Thou substance, soule and body to ingage
Is the ambition of thy best desires :
Foes forraine to resist, to quell their rage
　　How willingly would'st thou thy selfe despise,
　　Count loosing of thy goods a gainfull prize
　　Lavish thy blood and thy life sacrifice.

44.

But when God's love directly doth withstand
And where his lawes the contrary convince[1]
Wee must not breake the heavenly king's command
Whilst we do seeke to please an earthly prince :
　　The burdens they impose on us to beare
　　Our dutie is to suffer them : but where
　　Kings bid and God forbids we must forbeare.

45.

Behold the man whose valour once surmounted
In sacking Zion's mount (mount not so high
As men therein were haughty !) and accounted
Of worthies chiefe doth most unworthily :
　　Hee that to summe the people of the land
　　Withstood the King now with the King doth
　　　stand
　　Too buxome[2] for to finish his command.

---

[1] Cf. Wright's invaluable ' Bible Word-Book ' s. v.　G.
[2] Obedient.　G.

46.

Next morne when early Phœbus first arose
(Which then arose last in Vriah's sight)
Him Joab in the forfront did dispose
From whom the rest recoyled in the fight :
    Thus of his friends betray'd by subtill traine
    Assaulted of his foes with might and maine
    He lost his life, not conquerèd but slaine.

47.

His mangled body they expose to scorne`
And now each cravin coward dare defie him,
Outstaring his pale visage, which beforne[1]
Were palsy-strook, with trembling to come nigh
     him :
    Thus heartlesse hares with purblind eyes do
     peere
    In the dead lyon's pawes, yea dastard deere
    Over his heartlesse corps dare domineere.

---

[1] Sometimes spelled 'beforen'=before : Thus Spencer

    The time was once and may again retorn

    For ought may happen that hath been beforn.

                  [Shepherds K. 103.] G.

DAVID'S HEARTIE REPENTANCE.

1.

THE tongue of guiltlesse blood is never
  ti'd
   In the earth's mouth, and though the
 greedy ground
Her gaping crannies quickly did provide
To drinke the liquor of Vriah's wound
  Yet it with moanes bescatterèd the skies
  And the revoicing eccho, with replies
  Did descant on the playn-song of the cries.

2.

Hereat the Lord perceiving how the field
Hee sow'd with grace, and compast with an
  heape
Of many measures, store of sinnes did yeild
Where he expected store of thankes to reape,
  With flames of anger, furnace-like he burn'd:
  For patience long despis'd and lewdly spurn'd
  Is at the length to raging fury turn'd.

3.

Then all the creatures musterèd their traine
From angells vnto worms, the blinde did see
Their Lord disgrac't, whose honour to maintaine
Things wanting life most lively seeme to be ;
    Refusing all to serve man that refus'd
    To serve his God, all striving to be us'd
    To punish him, his Maker that abus'd.

4.

Please it your Highnes for to give me leave
I'le scorch the wretch to cinders said the Fire :
Send me said Aire, him Il'e of breath bereave ;
No quoth the earnest Water I desire
    His soylie sinnes with deluges to scoure ;
    Nay let my Lord quoth Earth imploy my
    power
    With yawning chapps I will him quick
    devour.

5.

Soone with a word the Lord appeas'd this strife
Injoyning silence till He did vnfold
That precious volume cald the Booke of Life
Which He the Printer priniledg'd of old
    Containing those He freely did imbrace :
    Nor ever would I wish an higher grace
    Than in this Booke to have the lowest place.

6.

Within this Booke hee sought for David's name
Which having found He proffered to blot
(And David surely well deserv'd the same
That did his nature so with sinne bespot
 Though none are blotted out but such as never
 Were written in : nothing God's love can
  sever ;
 Once written there are written there for ever.)

7.

Strait from His throne the Prince of Peace arose
And with embraces did His Father binde
Imprisoning his armes, He did so close
(As loving iyve on an oake did winde
 And with her curling flexures it betraile)
 His Father glad to finde His force to fayle
 Strugel'd as one not willing to prevaile.

8.

Thus then began the Spotlesse Lambe to speake
(One word of Whom would rend the sturdy
  rocke,
Make hammer-scorning adamant to breake,
And vnto sense perswade the senseles stocke,
 Yea God Himselfe that knowes not to repent
 Is made by His petitions penitent
 His Justice made with Mercy to relent.)

9.

Why doth my Father's fury burne so fierce?
Shall Persian lawes vnalterable stand?
And shall my Lord decree and then reverse,
Enact and then repeale, and counter-mand?
  Tender Thy credit, gracious God, I crave
  And kill not him Thou didst conclude to save
  Can these hands blot what these hands did
    ingrave?

10.

Hath not Thy wisdom from eternity
Before the worlds foundation first was lay'd
Decree'd, the due time once expir'd, that I
Should flesh become and man borne of a maide?
  To live in poverty and dye with paine
  That so Thy Sonne for sinners vilely slaine
  Might make vile sinners live Thy sonnes
    againe?

11.

Let Me, oh let Me Thy feirce wrath asswage
And for this sinner begg a full discharge :
What though hee justly doth provoke Thy
    rage?
Thy justice I will satisfie at large.
  If that the Lord of Life must murder'd bee
  Let mee intreat this murd'rer may goe free
  My meritts cast on him, his sinnes on Me.

12.

Thus speaking from His fragrant cloaths there
    went
A pleasant breath whose odour did excell
Myrrhe, aloes and cassia for sent
And all perfum'd His Father with the smell
    Whereat His smothèd face most sweetly smil'd
    And hugging in His arms His dearest child
    Return'd those welcome words, with voyce
    most milde.

13.

Who can so pleasing violence withstand?
Thy craving is the hauing a request
Such mild intreaties doe my heart command
The 'mends is made and pacifi'd I rest :
    As far as earth from heaven doe distant lye
    As east is parted from the westerne skye
    So far his sinnes are sever'd from Mine eye.

14.

Hereat the heavenly quire lift vp their voyce
Angells and saints imparadis'd combine
Vpon their golden vialls to rejoyce
To rayse the prayse of the celestiall Trine,
    All in their songs a sacred strife exprest
    Which could sing better and surpasse the rest
    All did surpasse themselves and sang the best.

15.

Then said the Fire my fury I recant
Life-hatching warmth I will for him provide :
If David's breathlesse lungs do chance to pant
Said Aire Il'e fanne them with a windy tide :
    With moisture Il'e, said Water, quench his heat
    And I his hunger quoth the Earth, with meat
    Of marrow, fatnesse and the flower of wheat.

16.

Thus when a lord long buried in disgrace
A king to former favour doth restore
With all respect the court doth him embrace
Fawning as fast as they did flowte before :
    Where smiles or frownes are but the bare
        reflexion
    Of the king's face, and like to this direction
    Where hee affects they settle their affection.

17.

Plaine-dealing Nathan presently was sent
Nathan, than whom was none more skill'd to
        lanch
A festred soule, and with a searching tent[1]
To sound the sore : more cunning none to stanch

---

[1] Roll of lint used in searching or purifying a wound.
Cf. my Glossary to Sibbes sv. G.

A bleeding-hearted sinner nor more kinde
With swadling cloaths of comfort for to binde
Vnjoynted members of a troubled minde.

18.

Hee did not flow with wealth which envye heeds
Nor yet was he with penury opprest :
Want is the cause from which contempt proceeds:
His meanes were in the meane, and that's the best.
    High hills are parcht with heate or hid with
      snow
    And humble dales sone drown'd, that lie too
      low
    Whilst happy graine on hanging hills doth
      grow.

19.

For sundry duties he did dayes devide
Making exchange of worke his recreation;
For prayer he set the precious morne aside,
The mid-day he bequeath'd to meditation :
    Sweete sacred stories he reserv'd for night
    To reade of Moses' meeknes, Sampson's might:
    These were his joy, these onely his delight.

20.

But now dispensing with his dayly taske
To Court he comes and wisely did invent

Vnder a parable his mind to maske
Seeming to meane nought lesse than what he
    meant,
    And lapwing-like round fluttering a-while
    With far-fetcht præface and a witty wile,
    Hee made the king himselfe for to beguile.

21.

Thus he that thought all mortall men to cheate
And with false shewes his secret sinnes to
    shade,
Was couzned by the innocent deceite
Of one plaine prophet, and directly made
    As he a judge sate on the bench, to stand
    At barr a prisoner, holding[1] up his hand
    But first condemned by his owne command.[2]

22.

Goe fond[3] affectors of a flanting straine
Whose sermons strike at sinnes with slenting
    blowes,
Give me the man that's powerfull and plaine
The monster Vice vnmaskèd to expose:

---

[1] 'Thou art the man.' F.

[2] 'The man that hath done this thing shal dye.' F.

[3] Foolish. G.

Sùch preachers doe the soule and marrow part
And cause the guilty conscience to smart
Such please no itching eares but peirce the
    heart.

23.

This made King David's marble minde to melt
And to the former temper to returne
Thawing his frozen breast, whenas he felt
The lively sparks of grace therein to burne
    Which vnder ashes cold were choakt before :
    And now hee weeps and wayles and sighs full
    sore
    Though sure such sorrow did his joy restore.

24.

So have I scene one slumber'd in a swound
Whose sullen soule into his heart did hye
His pensive friends soone heave him from the
    ground
And to his face life-water doe apply :
    At length a long-expected sigh doth strive
    To bring the wellcome newes, the man's alive
    Whose soule at last doth in each part arive.

25.

Then to his harpe he did himselfe betake
(His tongue-tide harpe, long gowne out of request)

And next to this his glory[1] must awake
The member he of all accounted best :
    Then with those hands which he for griefe did
      wring
    Hee also lightly striks the warbling string
    And makes one voice servo both to sob and
      sing.

26.

That heavenly voyce to heare, I more desire
Than Syrens sweetest songs, than musicke made
By Philomele chiefe of the wingèd quire :
Or him whose layes so pleasing, did perswade
    Stones for to lackey when he went before ;[2]
    Or that brave harper whom unto the shore
    His hackny dolphin safely did restore.[3]

---

[1] Tongue. G.   [2] Orpheus. G.   [3] Arion. G.

DAVID'S HEAVIE PUNISHMENT.

1.

MOST true it is when penitents by grace
Acquitted are, the pardon of their
sinnes
And punishments release do both imbrace
Like to a paire of vndivided twinns
 Parted they cannot be, they cleave so fast
 Yet when the tempest of God's wrath is past
 Still his afflicting hony-shower doth last.

2.

But let the Schooles these thorny points dispute
Whose searching sight can naked truth discry,
Skulking in errors arms, and are acute
Fine-fingred with distinctions to untye
 Knots more than Gordian, these men never
  mist
 The slender marke, like[1] those in whose left fist
 There did so much dexterity consist.

---

[1] Judges xx. 16. F.

3.

Meane time my Muse come see how prettily
The patient infant doth itself behave;
Infant but newly borne, now neare to dye,[1]
That from the cradle posted to the grave.
  See with what silent signes and sighes full faine
  Poore heart it would expresse where lies the
      paine
  Complaining that it knowes not to complaine.

4.

Stay cruell Death! thy hand for pitty hold!
Against some aged grand-sire bend thy bow
That now hath full twice forty winters told,
Whose head is silver'd o're with ages snow:
  Dash out this babe, out of thy dismall bill
  And in exchange let him thy number fill
  So may he life, his friends enjoy him still.

5.

These hands to hurt another never sought
Which cannot helpe themselves they are so
      weake;
His heart did never hatch a wanton thought,
His tongue did never lye that cannot speake:

---

[1] The death of King David's child.   F.

By wrong and violence he ne're did wrest
The goods wherewith his neighbour is possest
When strength scarse servs to suck the nurse's
        brest.

6.

But ah ! this infant's guilt from him proceeds
That knew the least when most he sought to
        know ;
Who most was nak't when cloathed in his
        weeds
Best cloathed then when naked he did goe :
    In vayne the wit of wisest men doth strive
    To cut off this intayle, that doth derive[1]
    Death unto all when first they are alive.

7.

As when a tender rose begins to blow
Yet scarse unswadled is, some wanton maide,
Pleas'd with the smell, allured vith the show
Will not reprive it till it hath display'd
    The folded leaves : but to her brest applies
    Th' abortive budd, where coffined it lye's
    Losing the blushing dye before it dies.

---

[1] Communicate, transmit.   G.

8.

So this babe's life, newly begun, did end
Which sure receiv'd the substance though not
   sign'd
With grace's scale : God freely doth attend
His ordinance, but will not be confin'd
   Thereto when 'tis not neglected nor despis'd
   They that want water are by fire baptiz'd
   Those sanctify'd that ne're were circumcis'd.

9.

Sweet babe one sabbath thou on earth didst see
But endless sabbaths doest in heaven survive :
Grant, Death of joyfull bowers depriv'd thee
Thou hadst seene yeares of sorrowes if alive :
   True thou wast borne a prince but now art
     crown'd
   A king by death; sleepe therefore in the ground
   Sweetly untill the trumpet last shall sound.

10.

By this child's death king David did sustaine
One losse : but where this misery did end
More miseries began : as in a chayne
One link doth on another linke depend :
   His lust with lust, his slaying with a slaughter
   Must punish't be : proportion'd therafter
   To mother sinne is punishment the daughter.

11.[1]

Amnon advis'd by Jonadab, a fit
Of sicknesse faines : men wickedly inclin'd
Worse counsellors (that with great store of wit
Have dearth of grace) most easily may find :
> And Thamar's hands his meate must onely
> make :
> Ah ! happy age when ladies learn't to bake
> And when kings daughters knew to knead a
> cake.

12.

Rebecka was esteem'd of comely hew
Yet not so nice her comelinesse to keepe
But that shee water for the cammells drew :
Rachell was faire, yet fedd her father's sheepe
> But now for to supply Rebecka's place
> Or doe as Rachell did is counted base :
> Our dainty dames would take it in disgrace.

13.

But quickly did his beastly lust declare
That he to eate her daynties had no neede :
He for the cooke not for the cates[2] did care
Shee was the dish on whom he meant to feed :

---

1 The deflouring of Thamar.   F.   2 Provisions.   G.

Oh how she pray'd and strove with might and
   maine
And then from striving fell to prayers againe :
But prayers and striving both alike in vaine.

14.

Thus a poore larke imprison'd in the cage
Of a kite claws most sweetly sings at large
Her owne dirge whilst she seeks to calm his rage
And from her jaylor sue's for a discharge :
   Who passing[1] for no musick that surpast
   To feede his eares whilst that his gutts doe fast
   On her that pray'd so long, doth prey at last.

15.

Then with dust-powder'd haire she sore bewayles
And punisht on herselfe her brother's sinne :
Parting her maiden livery with nayles
That parted was with colours, and wherein
   White streaks their owner's innocence did show
   The bashful red her modesty : the row
   Of sable sorrowed for the wearer's woe.

16.

Comfort thyselfe more virtuous than faire
More faire than happy virgin, mourn with measure

---

[1] 'Having regard for.'   G.

Sinnes unconsented to no soules impaire
That must be done perchance with bodies plea-
    sure
  Which with the grief of soull may be constrain'd :
  The casket broke the jewell still remain'd
  Vntoucht which in the casket was contain'd

17.

In his brest[1] Absalom records this wrong :
Out of our minds good turnes doe quickly passe
But injuries therein remaine too long
Those scrawl'd in dust but these ingrav'd in
    brasse :
  One sunset for our anger should suffice
  Which in his wrath set oft, oft did arise
  With yearly race surrounding twice the skies.

18.

Now when his fruitfull flocks which long had
    worne
Their woolen coates for to make others hot
Were now to forfeit them, and to be shorne
(Sure from the silly sheepe his divelish plott
  Their owner never learn'd) hee finds a way
  To worke revenge, and callèd on that day
  His brothers to a feast which prov'd a fray.

---

[1] The murdering of Amnon. F.

19.

What Amnon drunke in wine in blood he spilt
Which did the dainties marre and meate defile
Cupps, carpetts, all with goary streaks were gilt
Seeming to blush that cruely so vile
    So fowly savage should the banquet staine:
    Thus he that being well did sicknesse faine
    Not being sicke was on a suddenne slaine.

20.

The rest refused on the meate to feede
Whose bellies were so full with griefe and feare
To feele what they had seene: away they speed
To ride: but Fame did fly, Fame that doth weare
    An hundred listning eares, an hundred eyes;
    An hundred prating tongues, she dayly plies
    Tongues that both tell the truth and tattle lyes.

21.

She gets by going and doth gather strength
As balls of snow by rolling more doe gaine
She whisp'rd first but lowdly blaz'd at length
All the kings sonnes, all the kings sonnes are
    slaine:
    The pensive Court in dolefull dumps did rue
    This dismall case till they the matter knew:
    Would all bad news like this might prove
    untrue.

22.

Goe silly soules that doe so much admire
Court curious intertainment and fine fare
May you for mee obtaine what you desire
I for your fowles of Phasis[1] do not care
    If that such riots at your feasts be rife
    And all your meate so sowrely sauc'd with strife
    That guests to pay the shot must lose their life.

23.

Happy those swaines that in some shady bower
Making the grasse their cloath, the ground their
      board
Doe feede on mellow fruite or milk's fine flower
Vsing no wine but what their wells afford:
    At these did malice never bend her bow
    Their state is shot free, it is set so low
    They overlooke that would them overthrow

24.

Fast unto Geshure flies the fratricide
To shelter there himselfe; the sentence sore
Of angry justice fearing to abide :
Oh happy turne had he return'd no more

---

[1] That is 'pheasants:' the bird having been introduced into Europe from Phasis on the coast of the Euxine: hence *phasianæ aves:* Aristophanes, Acharn 726: Pliny N.H. &c. &c.   G.

Who wonted guise kept in a country strange:
Those that abroad to forraine parts do range
Their climate not conditions doe exchange.

25.

Return'd: at entrance of the Court[1] he stands
If any sutors there he chanc't to finde
Hee steales their hearts by taking of their hands
And suckèd out their soule with kisses kinde:
　He of their name, cause, citty doth inquire:
　Proud men prove base to compasse their desire
　They lowest crouch that highest doe aspire.

26.

Before such kisses come vpon my face
Oh let the deadly scorpion me sting
Yea rather than such armes should me imbrace
Let curling snakes about my body cling:
　Than such faire words I'de rather the fowle
　Vntuned schreeching of the dolefull owle
　Or heare the direfull mountaine-wolfe to howle.

27.

Some men affirme that Absalom doth sound
In the worlds oldest tongue ['of' peace a father']

---

[1] Absalom's aspiring to the kingdom. F.

But certs I know that such mistake their ground:
['Rebellious sonne'] sure it importeth rather:
 And yet why so? sith[1] since I call to minde
 Than the *clementes* none were more unkind
 Than *innocent* more nocent none I finde.[2]

28.

Then borrowing the plausible disguise
Of holinesse he mask't his plot so evill
Vnder the good pretence of sacrifice
(A saint dissembled is a double devill)
 But sure were those the vowes he went to pay
 His sire, that harmelesse sheepe he vow'd to slay
 Who o're mount Olivet weeping fled away

29.

This makes mee call my Saviour's griefe to minde
Who on[3] this mount because the Jewes were
   growne
So wicked: those that said they saw so blind—
Mourn'd for their sins that mourn'd not for their
   own:
 Much did He weepe for others that forbad
 Others to weepe for Him, whose being sad
 Hath made his saints for ever since full glad.

---

[1] Cf. Wright, as before s. v.   G.
[2] The Popes so (mis)-named.   G.   [3] Luke xix. 42.   F.

30.

Downe comes the king to Jordan : on the sand
If that the saylors chance to ground the boat
A flood of teares they straitwayes did command
Whose large accession made the vessell floate :
 And if a blaste of winde did chance to faile
 So greivously the people did bewayle
 Their very sighs might serve to stuffe the sayle.

31.

Thus was the king on his own land exil'd
His subjects were his hoast and he their guest
Whose place was ill supplied by his child
(Vnhappy bird defiling his owne nest)
 That tooke his fathers wives, in open sight:
 Those that do want of grace the sunshine
 bright
 Extinguish't oft dim nature's candle light.

32.

The blushing sun no sooner did behold
So beastly lust but sought his face to shrowd
And shrinking in his beames of burnish't gold
Was glad to skulke within a sullen cloud :
 The shamefac't birds with one wing faine
 to fly
 Did hold their other fanne before their eye
 For feare they should such filthinesse espie.

33.

What needed he to keepe alive his name
Erect a pillar?   Sure this damned deed
Makes us remember and detect the fame
That in the world's last doating age succeed :
 Yea when that brasse that seemeth Time to
  scorne
 Shall be by all-devouring Time out-worne
 His name they'le beare in minde that are not
  borne.

34.

But[1] he that gave this counsell did not speed
Who speeding home on witlesse asse amaine
(Asse that for wit his rider did exceed)
Cause he his will at Court could not obtaine
 Did make his will at home : the peevish elfe
 Amongst his houshold, parts his cursed pelfe
 Carefull of that but carelesse of himselfe.

35

Oh ! suddaine thought of thy mortality !
Thou art not yet so thorough worne with age,
Nor in thy face such symptoms can espy
Which should so neare approaching death pre-
 sage :

---

[1] Ahithophel hanging himselfe.   F.

Thy state is not distempered with heate
Thy working pulse doth moderately beate
All outward things seeme whole, seeme all
   compleate.

36.

But ghostly is thy griefe : Thou that by treason
Against thy leige so lately wast combin'd
Thy passions now rebell against thy reason
Reason that is the soveraigne of thy minde
   And seeke for to disturbe it from the throne :
   Strive, strive to set these civill broyles at one
   Order thyselfe and let thy house alone.

37.

A chayne of hempe he to his necke made fast   _Turns_
By tying of which knot hee did untye
The knot of soule and body, and at last
Stopping the passage of his breath, thereby
   A passage for his soule, wide opened hee :
   Thus traytors rather than they should goe free
   Themselves the hangmen of themselves will bee.

38.

His friends to balm his body spare no cost
With spices seeking to perfume a sinke
For certs I know their labour was but lost :
His rotten memory will ever stinke

His soule thereby was nothing bettered
Because his corps were bravely buried:
Tombs please the living profit not the dead.

39.

How many worthy martyrs vilely slaine
Made meate for fowles or for the fire made fuell
Though ground they could not for a grave obtaine
Were not lesse happy but their foes more cruell:
Vnburied bodies made not them unblest
Their better halfe did find an heavenly rest
And doth injoy joyes not to be exprest.

40.

Leave us the traytor thus vpon whose hearsse
My Muse shall not a precious teare mispend
Proceeding to bemoane in dolefull verse
How[1] two great bands with cruell blowes con-
    tend:
Whole clouds of arrowes made the sky to lowre
Dissolv'd at length into a bloody showre
Till steele kill'd many, wood did more devoure.

41.

Oh let it not be publish't in the path
That leads unto th' incestuous seed of Lot

---

[1] The battell betwixt Absalom and David's men.   F.

Tell not these tidings in the towne of Gath
In Ascalon see ye proclaime it not
 Least these rejoyce at this calamity
 Who count your fame their greatest infamy
 Your wofull jarrs their welcome melody.

42.

Had Rachel now reviv'd her sonnes to see
Their bloody hands would make her heart to
  bleed
Each a Benoni unto her would be ;
Had Leah liv'd to see herselfe agree'd
 To fall out with herselfe, with teares, most sure
 She would have made her tender eyes past cure ;
 Who ever wonn she must the losse endure.

43.

The conquest (which her verdict long suspended)
Hover'd aloft not knowing where to light ;
But at the last the lesser side befreinded
With best successe : the other put to flight
 More trusted a swift foote than a strong fist
 Most voices oft of verity have mist
 Nor in most men doth victory consist.

44.

The gracelesse sonne was plung'd in deepe dis-
tresse

For earth his weight no longer would endure
The angry heavens denied all accesse
Vnto a wretch so wicked, so impure
    At last the heavens and earth with one con-
      sent
    A middle place vnto the monster lent
    Above the earth, beneath the firmament.

45.

His skittish mule ran roving in the fields
And up high hills, downe dales, o're woods did
      prance
Seeming with neighing noyse and wanton heeles
In token of great joy to sing and dance,
    That now her maister she should beare no
      more
    (An heavy bulke whose sinnes did weigh so
      sore)
    Now rid of him that rid on her before.

46.

Cry, Absalom, cry, Absalom, amaine,
And let thy wingèd prayers pierce the skye!
Oh to the spring of pitty soone complaine
That ne're is dammed up nor drained dry;
    Thy fault confesse, His favour eke implore
    Much is thy misery, His mercy more
    Thy want is great but greater is His store.

47.

Condemne thyselfe and He shall thee acquitt
Doe then but pray He'll pitty thy estate,
Confesse thy debt He will the same remit
It never was too soone, it's ne're too late :
   Alas : long sinners scarse at last relent
   Hee gives not all offenders to repent
   That granteth pardon to all penitent.

48.

Whilst thus his life suspended was on high
Bold-ventrous Joab opened his heart
(Heart where much treason lurked privily)
And peir'et his body with a triple dart :
   Then crimson blades of grasse whereon he
      bleeds
   Did straitwayes dye, and in their room succeeds
   A fruitfull wildernesse of fruitlesse weeds.

49.

When David heard the victory was gain'd
But his sonne lost (as Jordan waxing ranke
O're flowes the land and scornes to be restrain'd
To have his ti'de in a narrow banke)
   Surges of sorrow in his heart did rise
   And brake the watry sluces of his eyes
   Who lightned thus himselfe with heavy cryes :

F

50.

My sonne, whose body had of grace[1] the fill !
My sonne, whose soule was so devoid of grace ![2]
Without my knowledge and against my will
My sonne, in cause so bad, so strange a place :
  My sonne, my sonne for which I must com-
    plaine
  I feare in soule as in the body slaine
  Would I might dye that thou might'st live
    againe.

51.

Now when this griefe was swallow'd not digested
The subjects flock't king David to restore
Who in an instant love what they detested
Detest in th' instant what they lov'd before :
  People like weather-cocks wav'd with the wind
  We constant in inconstancy may finde
  As time counts minutes so they change their
    minde.

52.

Amongst the rest that came the king to meete
Lame-leg'd Mephibosheth, but loyall-hearted
Was one that never washt his cloaths or feete
(Except with teares) since David first departed ;

---

[1] 'Beauty.' G.   [2] That is 'goodness,' holiness. G.

Feete which by fall from nurse's armes began
To halt, with him a child so fast she ran
That he could never goe when growne a man.

53.

Not much unlike—if it give no distaste
That reall truths I doe with trifles match—
Whilst that my posting Muse, with headlong
       haste
Doth strive her rurall layes for to dispatch
    Halting invention, for the want of heede
    And lame unjoynted lines from her proceede :
    And seldome things done speedily doe speed.

54.

But here an vnexpected jarre arose
Whilst people for most part in [th'] prince con-
       tended ;
Which grew from bitter words to bloody
       blowes :
The king quoth Judah of our tribe descended
    Hee of our flesh is flesh, bone of our bone :
    Nay answer'd Israel in the king wee owne
    Ten parts, a single share is yours alone.

55.

Whilst sparks of discord thus began to smoake
To finde the bellowes Sheba did conspire

(Sheba[1] that proudly did disdaine the yoke)
And blowing of a trumpet, blew the fire :
　Then those that claimed ten disdain'd all
　　part
　In David, taught by his seducing art
　They discontented to their tents depart.

56.

This rebell Joab whilst to quell he strives,
A nameles woman (in the booke of life
Her name is kept that kept so many lives)
Procur'd that he who stirrèd up the strife
　The body of the common-wealth to rend
　From prince the head whereon it did depend
　With head from body rent his life did end.

57.

By his death many citizens surviv'd ;
The losse of traytors bloud did prove their gaine ;
Soone cea'st the flood of discord, thence deriv'd
When they the factions fountaine did restraine.
　This warre a vile man with[2] a word did
　　rayse
　Vnto his shame, which to her endlesse prayse
　A worthy woman with a word[3] allaies.

---

[1] 'The sonne of Belial.' F.
[2] 'What faith have we in David.' F.
[3] 'His head shall be thrown,' etc. F.

58.

So in our Land a noble queene arose,
As we have heard our fathers oft relate ;
A maide yet manly to confound her foes,
A maide and yet a mother to the State :
 Which she weake, like to crumbling bricke did
  finde,
 Which strong as lasting marble she resign'd
 Gold and God's worship both by her refin'd.

59.

She having flourishèd in great renowne
In spite of power and policy of Spaine,
Did change her earthly for an heavenly crowne
And cea'st to rule o're men, with God to
 raigne ;
 Fourty and foure Novembers fully past
 (Aie me that winged Time should post so
  fast)
 To Christ, her love, she wedded was at last.[1]

60.

This sunne thus set there followed no night
In our horizon ; strait another sunne
Most happily continued the light
Which by the first was hopefully begunne :

---

[1] Elizabeth. G.

And what might most amaze all mortall eyes
Never before out of the Northern skies
Did men behold bright Phœbus to arise.

61.

Arts did increase his fame, he did increase
The fame of arts ; and counting twice eleven
Twelve months upon his throne, this prince of
    peace
By falling to the earth did rise to heaven :
    Then downe our cheeks teares hot and cold did
    flow
    Those for the sire deceast exprest our woe,
    Those joy for his succeeding sonne did
    show.[1]

62.

Live gracious leige whose vertues doe surmount
All flattery, and envy them admires ;
Center of grace and greatnesse, live to count
Till that thy kingdom with the world expires :
    Wee subjects wish thee worst that love thee
    best
    Who here long to injoy thee, doe request
    That late thou mayst injoy an heavenly
    rest.[2]

---

[1] James I.   G.   [2] Charles I.   G.

63.

And thou young prince, hope of the future age
Succeed to fathers vertues, name and crowne ;
A new starre did thy Saviour's birth præsage
His death the sun eclipsèd did renowne :
 But both of these conjoynèd to adorne
 Thy wellcome birth, the sun with age so
  worne
 Did seeme halfe dead and a young starr was
  borne[1]

64.

But what dost thou my vent'rous Muse præsume
So far above thy dwarf-like strength to straine?
Such soaring soone will melt thy waxen plume ;
Let those heroike sparks whose learned braine
 Doth merit chapletts of victorious bayes •
 Make kings the subject of their lofty layes
 Thy worthlesse praysing doth their worth dis-
 praise.

65.

Strike saile, and to thy matter draw more neare
And draw thy matter nearer to an end :
Though nought prayse-worthy in thy verse
 appeare
Yet strive that shortnesse may the same commend :

---

[1] Charles II. G.

Returne to see where Joab homeward goes
To see his friends that had subdu'd his foes ;
His souldiers and himself there to repose.

66.

Thus when two adverse winds with strong com-
mand
Summon the sea, the waves that both do feele,
Dare follow neither but in doubt do stand,
Whilst that the shipps, with water drunke, doe
reele
With men, for grief of drowning drown'd in griefe
Vntill at length a calme brings them reliefe
And stills the storme that had so long been
briefe.

• 67.

Oh ! that I might but live tho see the day
(Day that I more desire then hope to see)
When all these bloody discords done away
Our princes in like manner might agree.
When all the world might smile in perfect peace
And these long-lasting broyls at length might
cease
Broyles which alas doe dayly more increase.

68.

The Netherlands with endlesse warrs are tost

Like in successe to their unconstant tide
Losing their gettings, gaining what they lost.
Denmarke both sword and Baltick seas divide :
   More blood than juice of grape nigh Rhine is
     shed
   And Brunswicke land will not be comforted
   But cryes my duke alas ! my duke is dead.

69.

The warrs in France now layd aside not ended
Are onely skimmèd over with a scarre
Yea haughty Alps that to the clouds ascended
Are over-climbèd with a bloody warre :
   And Maroes birth-place Mantua is more
   Made famous nor for Mars and battel sore
   Than for his muse it famèd was before.   •

70.

Sweden to stopp th' infernall flood provides
(May his good cause be crown'd with like successe ;
And they that now please none, to please both
     sides
May they themselves his trusty friends expresse)
   But Turks the cobweb of their truce each howre
   Doe breake ; they wayte a time but want no
     powre
   Nor will, warr-wearied Christians to devore.

71.

But let the cunning Chymicke whose exact
Skill caused light from darknesse to proceed ;
Out of disorder order can extract
Make in his due time all these jars agree'd,
   Whose greivances may be bemoan'd by men,
   By God alone redressed : and till then
   They more befitt my prayers than my pen.

ΤΩ ΜΟΝΩ ΔΟΞΑ ΘΕΩ.

FINIS.

II. PANEGYRICK ON HIS MAJESTIES HAPPY RETURN.[1]

1.

AT Wor'ster great God's goodness to
    our Nation
    It was a conquest, your bare pre-
        servation.
When 'midst your fierces foes on every side
For your escape God did a lane provide ;
They saw you gone, but whither could not tell
Star-staring, though they ask'd both heaven and
    hell.[2]

---

[1] A Panegyrick to His Majesty on his Happy Return.
By Tho. Fuller B.D. London, Printed for John Playford
at his shop in the Temple. 1660 [4°.] An earlier and very
much shorter version of the 'Panegyrick' appeared in the
'Worthies' under Worcestershire with these truly Fullerian
words 'And here my Muse craves her own *Nunc dimittis*,
never to make verses more : and because she cannot write
on a better, will not write on another occasion, but heartily
pray in prose for the happiness of her lord and master.
And now having taken our *Vale* of verses' . . . . G.

[2] 'Lane' (line 4th) is printed in large capitals LANE—
Why? 'His sacred Majesty escaped, by royal oaks and

2.

Of forreign States you since have studied store
And read whole libraries of princes o're.
To you all forts, towns, towers and ships are
     known
(But none like those which now become your
     own)
And though your eyes were with all objects fill'd
Onely the good into your heart distill'd.

3.

Garbling men's manners, you did well divide,
To take the Spaniard's wisdom not their pride:
With French activity you stor'd your mind
Leaving to them their ficklenesse behind;
And soon did learn, your temperance was such
A sober industry even from the Duch.[1]

4.

But tell us, gracious sovereign, from whence
Took you the pattern of your patience?

---

other miraculous appliances well known to mankind: but
Fourteen-thousand other men, sacred too after a sort though
not majesties, did not escape. One could weep at such a death
for brave men in such a Cause.' Carlyle's Cromwell: Battle
of Worcester: [Vol. iii. p. 200: edn 4 vols. 8vo 1850.]   G.

   [1] Well that winsome Fuller lived not to see his ideal
befouled and befouling.   G.

Learn't in affliction's School under the rod
Which was both us'd and sanctifi'd by God;
From Him alone that lesson did proceed,
Best tutor with best pupil best agreed.

5.

We your dull subjects must confess our crime
Who learnt so little in so long a time,
And the same School : thus dunces' poring looks
Mend not themselves but only marre their books.
How vast the difference 'twixt wise and fool !
The Master makes the schollar, not the school.

6.

With rich conditions Rome did you invite
Hoping to purchase you their proselyte
(An empty soul's soon tempted with full coffers)
Whilst you with sacred scorn refus'd their proffers:
And for the Faith did earnestly contend[1]
Abroad which now you do at home defend.

7.

Amidst all storms, calm to yourself the while,
Saddest afflictions you did teach to smile.

---

[1] Jude 3 'Contend for the faith which was once delivered
unto the saints.'   F

Some faces best become a mourning dress'
And such your patience, which did grace distress,
Whose soul, despising want of worldly pelf
At lowest ebbe went not beneath itself.

8.

God's justice now no longer could dispence
With the abusing of his Providence ;
To hear successe his approbation styl'd
And see the bastard brought against the child.
Scripture by such who in their own excuse
Their actings 'gainst God's writings did produce.

9.

The Independent doth the Papist shun
Contrary ways their violence doth run :
And yet in such a round at last they met
That both their saints for mediators set :[1]
We were not ripe for mercy, God he knows
But ready for his justice were our foes.

10.

The pillar which God's people did attend
To them in night a constant light did lend,

---

1 Witness a sermon. F. [Query—Dr Thomas Goodwin
and Peter Sterry ? The famous 'prayer' of the former so
perverted in one expression therein, doubtless simply used
Jeremiah's sorrowful plaint: Jeremiah xx. 7. G.

Though dark unto th' Egyptians behind;
Such was brave Monck:[1] in his reservèd mind
A riddle to his foes he did appear
But to himself and you, sense plain and clear.

11.

By means unlikely God atchieves his end
And crooked wayes straight to his honour tend;
The great and ancient gates of London town
(No gates no city) now are voted down
And down were cast, O happy day! for all
Do date our hopeful rising from their fall.

12.

The matter of your Restitution's good
The manner better, without drop of blood:
By a dry conquest, without forreign hand
Self-hurt and now self-healèd is our Land.
This silent turn did make no noise, O strange!
Few saw the changing—all behold the change.

13.

So Solomon most wisely did contrive
His temple should be still-born though alive.
That stately structure started from the ground
Unto the roof, not guilty of the sound

---

[1] See Carlyle, as above, *sub nomine*. G.

Of iron tool, all noise therein debarr'd :
This virgin-Temple thus was seen not heard.

14.

When two Protectors were of late proclaim'd
Courting men's tongues, both miss't at what they
 aim'd :
True English hearts did with just anger burn
And would no echo of ' God save ' return :
Though smiling silence doth consent imply
A tongue-tied sorrow flatly doth deny.[1]

15.

But at your majestie's first proclamation
How loud a stentor did invoice our nation !
A mouth without a tongue was sooner found
In all that crowd than tongue without a sound :
Nor was't a wonder men did silence break
When conduits did both French and Spanish
 speak.[2]

---

[1] The 'two Protectors' alluded to were Oliver Cromwell and Richard Cromwell. It need scarcely be said that
it is a Royalist delusion that in either case but specially in
that of Oliver the national ' welcome ' was less real or less
warm than that to Charles II. G.

[2] The ' *Wines* ' of Spain and France 'ran' from the
' fountains ' of the city. G.

16.

The bells aloud did ring for joy : they felt
Hereafter sacriledge shall not them melt.
The bonfires round about the streets did blaze
And these new lights fanatiques did amaze :
The brandisht swords this boon begg'd before death
Once to be shew'd then buried in the sheath.

17.

The Spaniard looking with a serious eye
Was forc'd to trespass on his gravity
Close to conceal his wond'ring he desir'd
But all in vain who openly admir'd.
The French who thought the English mad in mind
Now fear too soon they may them sober find.

18.

The Germans seeing this your sudden power
Freely confess another emperour.
The joyful Dane to heav'ns cast up his eyes
Presuming suffering kings will sympathize.
The Hollanders—first in a sad suspence—
Hop'd that good mercy was their innocence.

19.

As aged Jacob with good news intranc'd
That Joseph was both living and advanc'd :

The great surprize so deeply did prevail
On the good patriarch that his heart did fail :
Too little for to lodge so large a joy—
For sudden happiness may much annoy.

20.

But when he saw—with serious intent
To fetch him home—the waggons his son sent
That cordial soon his fainting heart did cure
'Twas past suspicion, all things then were sure :
The father his old spirits did renew
And found his fears were false, his joyes were true.

21.

Such our condition : At the first express
We could not credit our own happiness ;
Told of the coming of your majesty
Our fainting hearts did give their tongues the lye
A boon too big for us—so ill we live—
For to receive though not for God to give.

22.

But when we saw the royal Fleet at Dover
Voted to wait and waft your highness over
And valient Montague—all vertue's friend[1]—
Appointed on your person to attend :

---

[1] See note to dedication of 'David's Hainous Sinne,'
p. 35. G.

Joy from that moment did expell our grief
Converted into slow but sure belief.

23.

Th' impatient land did for your presence long :
England in swarms did into Holland throng
To bring your highness home, by th' Parliament
Lords, Commons, Citizens, Divines were sent :
Such honour subjects never had before
And hope that never any shall have more.

24.

With all degrees your carriage accords
Most lord-like your reception of the lords :
Your answer with the Commons so comply'd
They were to admiration satisfi'd ;
Civil the citizens you entertain'd—
As if, in London born, y'ad there remain'd.

25.

But oh ! your short, but thick expressive lines
Which did both please and profit the Divines :
Those pastors when returnèd to their charge
For their next sermon had your words at large
With some notes for your practice, who can
        teach
Our miters by your living what to preach.

26.

The States of Holland (or Low Countries now)
Unto your sacred majesty did bow :
What air, what earth, what water could afford
Best in the kind, was crowded on their board :
And yet when all was done, the royal guest
And not the chear ; he, he did make the feast.

27.

Th' officious wind to serve you did not fail
But scour'd from west to east to fill your sail
And fearing that his breath might be too rough
Prov'd over-civil and was scarce enough ;
Almost you were becalm'd amidst the main
Prognostick of your perfect, peaceful reign.

28.

Your narrow seas forreigners do wrong
To claim them—surely doth the ditch belong
Not to the common continent but isle
Inclosed—did on you their owner smile :
Not the least loss, onely the Naseby mar'ls
To see herself now drowned in the Charles.

29.

You land at Dover, shoals of people come
And Kent alone now seems all Christendom.

The Cornish rebels, eight score summers since
At Black-heath fought against their lawful prince
Henry the Seventh, which place with treason
    stain'd,
Its credit now, by loyalty regain'd.

30.

Great London the last station you did make
You took not it but London you did take :
Where some who sav'd themselves amongst the
    croud
Did lose their hearing, shoutings were so loud.
Now at Whitehall the guard which you attends
Keeps out your foes : God keep you from your
    friends.

31.

Thus far fair weather on your work attended
Let showres begin now where the sunshine ended.
Next day we smil'd at th' weeping of the skies
With all concerns how Providence complies !
The city serv'd, next followeth the village
And trading quickned, God provides for tillage.

32.

One face, one forme in all the Land appears
All, former foot now hors'd to cavaliers.
As for your enemies their cursed crew

Are now more hard to find out than subdue.
'Tis very death to them they cannot dye
Who do know whence not whither for to flie.

33.

France flouts, Spain scorns and Italy denies
 them
Any access : the Dane with Dutch defies them ;
Unto New England they were known of old
And now no footing for them on that mold.
Rich Amsterdam—the staple of all sects
These bankrupt rebels with contempt rejects.

34.

Thus cruell Cain who pious blood first spilt
Was pursevanted[1] after by his guilt,
With murderer imbranded on his face
Kept his condition though he chang'd his place :
Wand'ring from land to land, from shore to
 shelf
His guilty soul nere wandered from itself.

35.

Let them themselves in unknown lands disperse
Or if they please with canibals converse,
Like unto like, that all the world may see

---

[1] Followed as by 'pursuivant.' G.

King-killers and men-eaters do agree :
In no land they'l increase, 'tis nature's love
Unto mankind : all monsters barren prove.

36.

Long live our gracious Charles second to none
In honour, who ere sate upon the throne :
Be you above your ancestors renown'd,
Whose goodness wisely doth your greatness
    bound ;
And knowing that you may be what you
    would
Are pleased to be onely what you should.

37.

Europ's great arbitrator, in your choice
Is plac'd of Christendom the casting voice ;
Hold you the scales in your judicious hand
And when the equal beam shall doubtful
    stand,
As you are pleased to dispose one grain,
So falls or riseth either France or Spain.

38.

As Sheba's queen defective fame accus'd
Whose nigardly relations had abus'd
Th' abundant worth of Solomon, and told
Not half of what she after did behold :

The same your case, fame hath not done you
    right
Our ears are far out-acted by our sight.

39.

Your self's the ship return'd from forreign
    trading
England's your port, experience the lading,
God is the pilot; and now richly fraught
Unto the port the ship is safely brought:
What's dear to you is to your subjects cheap
You sav'd with pain, what we with pleasure reap.

40.

The most renowned Edward the Confessor
Was both your parallel and predecessor,
Exil'd he many years did live in France
—From low foundations highest roofs advance—
The yoak in youth with patience he bore
But in his age the crown with honour wore.

41.

The common law, to him, the English owe
On whom a better gift you will bestow:
That which he made by you shall be made good
That prince and people's rights both understood
Both may be bankt in their respective station;
Which dare no fear of future inundation.

42.

Oppression, the king's evil, long indur'd
By others caus'd, by you alone thus cur'd :
God onely have the glory, you the praise
And we the profit by our peaceful dayes,
All forreigners the pattern for their State
To anoy rather than to imitate.

FINIS.

III. 'Verses' prefixed to the Scintilla Altaris of Edward Sparke D.D.[1]

(a) ON THE WORTHY WORK OF MY RESPECTED FRIEND ED. SPARKE D.D.

HEN pious Asa with his fathers slept
How solemnly his funerals they
kept !
A curious bed's contriv'd by art's devices

---

[1] The following is the full title-page of the book in the edition of 1678 :—

☞ ΟΥΣΙΑΣΤΗ'ΡΙΟΝ vel Scintilla Altaris. Primitive Devotion in the Feasts and Fasts of the Church of England. By Edward Sparke D.D., Chaplain in Ordinary to His Majesty. The sixth edition, Revised by the Author. With Additions upon the Three Grand Solemnities last annexed to the Liturgy: consisting of prose, poems, prayers and sculptures. London, Printed by T. Hodgkin for T. Basset and H. Brome at the George near St Dunstans in Feet-street and at the Gun at the West-end of St Pauls, 1678,' cr. 8vo.

Fuller's step-mother was daughter to Rob. Sparke: 'Coll. Regal. 1557. Rob. Sparke electus scholaris, postea Theol. Bac. Rector de Burbage in comitatu Ley-cestr novercæ meæ (quæ tamen amore verissima mater fuit) charissimus pater' Fuller's MS. in Jesus College, cited by Baker, M.S. vi. 275. G.

Fill'd all with Indian gums, Arabian spices.
This bed the case, wheroin his corps, the jewel
Is[1] for the burning[2] made the precious fuel
As if that Asa's body did aspire
To meet his soul and mount up in that fire.
Dead saints dead days now put into their urn :
See here a sweeter, brighter flame doth burn
Kindled from Holy SPARKS when[3] doth arise
No smoak to hurt, save only envious eyes :
Whilst my admiring Muse at distance stands
Desiring at his flame to warm her hands ;
Wherewith emboldened nearer she presumes
To steal a s[c]ent of these thy sweet perfumes.
But I recant my words and pardon crave
That I compar'd thy book unto the grave
Or urn of saints : for by thy pen's perfection
Saints are not buried but have resurrection.
The cozening witch in counterfeit disguise
Made but a seeming Samuel to rise ;
(Whom cunningly she did with mantle hide
To cloak her cheat, which else might be espide :)
But who will not thy worthy Work applaud ?
No falshood here, no forgery or fraud ;
Thou really dost from the dust retrive
And make not one but all saints to revive.

---

[1] Misprinted 'are.' G.   [2] 2 Chronicles xvi. 14. F
[3] Query 'whence'? G.

Yea by the pains which thou on them expends
Easter doth rise, Ascension-day ascends ;
Thy poetry is pleasant, pictures fine
Thy prose profound, but oh the prayers divine !
Thus hast thou pleased us in every part
Our fancies, judgments, with our eyes and heart.

(β) ON MY WORTHY FRIEND
DR SPARKE, HIS LEARNED BOOK.

BROOD of legendary saints of old
Were[1] hatched in heads both bald
and bold :
Some saints in nature ne'r had face or features
But only were their wild inventors creatures ;
As mountain-like St Christopher thy glory
No mole-hill yet of truth in all the story.
Sure hard his face who told such lies so oft !
But who believes them sure his head is soft :
Fiction of saints ne'er coyn'd so great a store
But faction in our age hath minted more :
Commend themselves, and there is half their
        trade ;
Condemn all others, then the saint is made.
    But here my friend presents a noble breed
Of ancient saints, such as were saints indeed :

---

[1] Misprinted 'where.'   G.

And yet these saints in these our iron times
When piety and learning both were crimes
Have had their Feasts and Fasts put down out-
  right
And all their days extinct in envious night :
Only the faithful fairs[1] did them retain :
Exil'd the Church i' th' town they do remain.
But O how much doth this thy labour merit
In these dead days thou put'st a quick'ning
  spirit :
For us thou writ'st, for us thou tak'st this toy'l,
To make us see this SPARKE[2] doth spend his
  oyl,

---

[1] = 'fair' ladies. G.

[2] With reference to Fuller's characteristic and inevitable
playing on the name of 'Sparke' it may be allowed me to
record here an amusing coincidence that chanced in Scotland
and the authenticity of which is beyond doubt—A clergyman (in Scotland) was called upon to administer the
ordinance of baptism to the child of a brother-clergyman
whose name was 'Sparke,' who had already a very large
family, with very short intervals between each.—After the
rite it is usual in Scotland—among Presbyterians—to sing
one of the versified Psalms or Paraphrases—and on the
occasion in question the officiating clergyman selected with
unconscious patness and to the excitement of the risibilities
of his audience and the consternation of his clerical friend,
the 5th Paraphrase, reading out *ore rotundo*, the second
verse—

'As SPARKS in *close succession* rise, etc. G.

Live learned pen, converse with men below
Some forty winters until ages' snow
Candy thy reverend locks, and make them look
White as thy soul and paper of thy book:
But when that bankrupt nature shall deny
To pay more moisture and when thou must dye.
Mount gallant soul with saints in bliss survive
Whose rites thy pen did in sad times retrive.

IV. From ' Genethliacum illustrissimorum Prin-
cipum Caroli et Mariæ a Musis Cantabrigiensi-
bus celebratum. 1631. [4°].

AD SERENISSIMUM REGEM.

Filia nata tibi sub quarta luce Novembris,
    Quintáque famosa est proditione dies.
Septima post decimam sceptris sacratur Elisæ,
    Nona ortu Rex est inclyte clara tuo.
A Jano incipiet noster non amplius annus ;
Tu manda, & primus jure November erit.

Tho. Fuller, Coll. Sid. Suff.[1]

---

1 In this volume there are 'Verses' by Milton's ' Edm.
King: Coll. Christi, Socius' (p. 39)—Barnabas Oley (pp.
57-62) - Jo. Randall (page 87). C.

V. From 'Rex Redux' (Cantab 1633), p. 55.

SCOTIÆ & ANGLIÆ MUTUA DISCEPTATIO.

Nunquid ut exires venisti, Carole? nunquid
—*Scotia.*
Major natali non mora danda solo?
Nunquid in sternum discedis Carole? nunquid
—*Angl.*
Immemor Arctoo Phœbus in orbe manet?
Parcus adeŏ, mensiŏque dies vix ima videtur,
—*Scot.*
Visa dies lætœ vix brevis hora mihi.
Longus abes, brevis hora dies, lux singula mensis,
—*Angl.*
Hic visus miseræ secula multa mihi.

REGINA AD REGEM.

Æqua fero viduis thalamis quòd sola jacebam :
Causa fuit vestræ digna corona moræ.
Quot menses absis, nova tot diademata sume :
Viliùs haud Regem terra emet ulla meum.

Thom. Fuller, Coll. Sid.

VI. From 'Ayres and Dialogues for One, Two and Three Voyces. By Henry Lawes, Servant to his late Matie in his publick and private Musick. London, Printed by T. H. for John Playford and are to be sold at his shop in the inner Temple near the Church door 1653' folio—[page 36].

AN ECCHO.

Imbre lachrymarum largo genas spargo, quavis
    au-rorâ,
Deus citò tu venito, nunc nunc sine mora, ora :
Hoc non valet, semper oro, semper ploro cor de-
    ficit dolendo ;
Te te amo ad te clamo, dato finem flendo endo.
Peccatorum primus ego, hoc non nego, fateor vero :
Sed tu Deus esto meus, in te solum spero, ero :
Vox pergrata satis, satis, jam cedam fatis ; mor-
    tuus : vivam tamen :
Hic cum morior, cœlo orior, magnum magnum hoc
    solamen. Amen.

VII. In the Church-History[1] and 'Worthies' and indeed into all his books FULLER delights to introduce those *bits* of biographic fact and cha-

---

[1] The Church History of Britain : from the Birth of Jesus Christ until the year M.DC.XLVIII. Endeavoured by Thomas Fuller. London 1655 folio.

racter that are found in inscriptions on old
brasses and other monuments in old cathedrals
and in old, gray Churches and old books. He
usually translates them as well as the snatches of
Latin verse from 'Collections' of the Universities
and the like. Sometimes he does it under protest
and sometimes refuses quaintly *e.g.* on King
Lucius's epitaph he says it had nothing in it
'worthy of translation' and then with irrepressible wit goes on ' It seems the puddle-poet did
hope that the jingling of his rhyme would drown
the sound of his false quantity. Except any will
say that he affected to make the middle syllable
in *idola* short, because in the days of King Lucius,
idolatry was curb'd and contracted, whilst Christianity did dilate and extend itself.' [C. H. Book
I. Cent. III. page 15]. These Verse-Translations
make up the remainder of our Collection from
Fuller's published Works. Such as are original
not translated have a † after the number. With
two slight exceptions all the others are from the
Latin. The reader is referred to the several places
for the Original. In a few cases I give the Latin
along with the translation. G.

1. *Alban:* martyr

Here Alban, Rome ! thy citizen renown'd
With rosy grace of martyrdom was crown'd.
　　　[Book I. Cent. iv. page 17].

2. *St German:*

O thou that twice pierc'd Britain, cut asunder
From the whole world, twice didst survey the
　　wonder
Of monstrous seas :—
　　　[Book I. Cent. v. page 31.]

3. *On a woman who would enter a Church
from which women were excluded:*

They build a Church where women may not enter
One try'd but lost her life for her adventure.
　　　[Book II. Cent. vi. page 53].

4. *Easter in Britain:*

No writings fond[1] we follow, but do hold
Our country course, which Polycarp of old,
Scholar to blessed John, to us hath given.
For he, when th' moon had finish'd days twice
　　seven,
Bad us to keep the holy Paschal time
And count dissenting for an hainous crime.
　　　[Book II. Cent. vii. page 69].

---

[1] Foolish. G.

5. *Lines from the Welsh of Taliesen (?).*[1]

Wo be to that Priest y-born
That will not cleanly weed his corn,
And preach his charge among :
Wo be to that Shepheard (I say)
That will not watch his fold alway
As to his office doth belong.
Wo be to him that doth not keep
From Romish wolves his sheep
With staffe and weapon strong.
[Book II. Cent. vii. page 69].

---

[1] For *above*, read more accurately Taliesin: and cf.
Abp. Ussher's 'Religion anciently professed by the Irish
and British (1861) c. X.: Elrington's Ussher Vol. iv. 353.
On this Dr S. P. Tregelles writes me as follows:—"Ussher
calls the writer Taliessyn, and he uses the lines to 'shew
that he wrote after the coming of Austin into England, and
not fifty or sixty years before, as others have imagined.' I
however should use the contents of the lines, as shewing
that Taliesin cannot be the author; and indeed an old
Welsh copy ascribes them to 'Jonas the teacher of St
Davids' (? 10th century). The later that they are, the more
remarkable is the testimony against Rome in the ancient
British Church, the origin of which belongs to a time when
Ireland and Scotland were still in idolatry." After pointing
out mistakes in the Welsh as given by Ussher and Fuller
he adds, 'The poem from which the lines incorrectly as-
cribed to Taliesin are taken, is given in p. 78 col. 2 of the
new edition of the Welsh Archaiology, now in course of
publication at Denbigh.' G.

6. *On   the   Foundation   of   University   of Cambridge.*

Grant[1] long ago a city of great fame
From neighbouring river doth receive her name.
When storms of Saxon-warres her overthrew
Near to the old sprang up another new.
Monk Felix, whils't he Sigebert obeys
Light'ned this place with Schools and Learning's
     rayes.
Searching the monuments of British nation
This I assert in Grant's due commendation.

     [Leland : Book II. Cent. vii. page 75].

     7. *Victory of Oswald.*   'Amongst the many victories atchieved by this Oswald, one most re-markable was gained by him near Hex[h]am in Northumberland, against the Pagans, against whom he erected the standard of the Crosse, in a place which time out of mind was called *Heafen-field (Halcdon* at this day[2]) : by a prolepsis, not answering the name thereof until this time. Hence a Poet writing the life of Oswald [says]:—

Then he began the reason first to know
Of Heafen-feld, why it was calléd so ;

---

     ¹ Granta. G.   ² Scott's Halidon-hill. G.

Nam'd by the natives long since by foresight
That in that field would hap an heavenly fight.
[*Anony:* Book II. Cent. vii. page 78].

8. *On Oswald.*—'Whereupon Aidan laying
hold on Oswald's right hand (and that alone we
know ought to be the almoner [Matthew vi. 3]
'May this hand' (said he) 'never be consumed:'
which is said accordingly to come to passe.'

No worm, no rottennesse taints his right hand:
Corruption-free, in vain the cold doth strive
To freeze, or heat to melt it, which doth stand
Still at one stay: and though dead, is alive.

FULLER slyly adds, 'But it is not enough for us
that we have the poet's pen for it: if we also
had Oswald's hand to shew for the same, much
might be wrought on our behalf herein.'
[Book II. Cent. vii. page 82].

9. *On ' Wilfride's deprivation of the ' Bishop-
rick of York'* to which he had been appointed.
Boldly in the husband's life
Away from him they took his wife.

' But by the poet's leave, York was but espoused
not married to Wilfride, whilst he was in England: and after his going over beyond Sea, he

stayed so long that his Church presumed him
dead and herself a maid-widow, which lawfully
might receive another husband.'
[Book II. Cent. vii. page 86].

10. *Adelme, Bishop of Sherborn.* [He] 'was
the first of our English nation who wrote in
Latine : and the first that taught Englishmen to
make Latine verse, according to his promise,

If life me last, that I do see that native soile of
mine
From Aon top I'll first with me bring down the
Muses nine.
[Book II. Cent. viii. page 95].

11. *On 'Alba, since Rome,' from Aeneid
(lib. 3).*

Where under oakes on shore there shall be found
A mighty sow, all white, cast on the ground,
With thirty sucking piggs : that place is 'sign'd
To build your town and ease your wearied mind.
[Book II. Cent. viii. page 96].

12. *Martyrdom of King Edmond :* 'After
many indignities offered unto him they bound
him to a tree, and because he would not re-
nounce his Christianity, shot him with arrow

after arrow : their cruelty taking deliberation
that he might the better digest one pain before
another succeeded, so distinctly to protract his
torture (though confusion be better than method
in matters of cruelty) till not mercie but want of
a mark made them desist: according to the
poet's expression

Room wants for wounds but arrows do not fail
From foes, which thicker fly than winter hail.

The Latin is vivid

Jam loca vulneribus desunt, nec dum furiosis
Tela, sed hyberna grandine plura volant.
[Book II. Cent. ix. page 115].

13. *Of Alfred and Edward.*

If that it happ't that *conquered* was he
Next day to fight he quickly did prepare ;
But if he chanc't the *conquerour* to be,
Next day to fight he wisely did beware.
[Book II. Cent. ix. page 122].

14. DUNSTAN : ' Eminency occasions envy,
which made Dunstan's enemies endeavour to
depresse him. He is accused to the king for a
magician and upon that account banished the
Court. It was brought as evidence against him

that he made his harp not onely to have motion but made musick of itself, which no white-art could perform

> St Dunstan's harp fast by the wall
> Vpon a pin did hang-a :
> The harp itself, with ly and all
> Vntouch't by hand did twang-a.

For our part let Dunstan's harp hang there still, on a double suspicion twisted together : first, whether this story thereof were true or false : secondly, if true, whether done by magick or miracle. Sure I am, as good a harper and a better saint than Dunstan was, hath no such miracle reported of him, even David himself, who with his harp praised God, pleased men, frighted devils ; yet took pains with his own right hand [Psalm 137. 5] to play, not lazily commanding musick by miracle to be made on his instrument.'

[Book II. Cent. x. page 128].

[Strange, quick-witted FULLER did not think of the Æolian harp, wind-played—which doubt-less the poor accused saint's instrument was transformed into, accidentally. G.]

15. *The good daughter of a bad father :* ' Grant queen Edith a chast woman as she is

generally believed : daughter she was to a wicked father, Earle Godwin by name, whence the proverb

From prickly stock as springs a rose
So Edith from Earle Godwin grows.

little ill being written of the daughter and no good of the father.'
[Book II. Cent. xi. page 142].

16. *On Francis I.* ' *captive in Spain.*'

The captive King the Evil cures in Spain ;
Dear, as before, he doth to God remain.

' So it seemeth his medicinall quality is affixed not to his prosperity but person.'
[Book II. Cent. xi. page 147].

17. *On translations of Scripture* ' *The Originall preferred :*' ' Ricemarch a Britan, a right learned and godly clerk, son to Sulgen, bishop of St David's, flourishing in this age, made this epigram on those who translated the Psalter out of the Greek : so taking it at the second-hand and not drawing it immediately out of the first vessel '—

This harp the holy Hebrew text doth tender
Which, to their power, whils't every one doth
    render

In Latine tongue with many variations
He clouds the Hebrew rayes with his translations.
Thus liquors when twice shifted out, and pour'd
In a third vessel, are both cool'd and sour'd.
But holy Jerome truth to light doth bring
Briefer and fuller, fetch't from the Hebrew
    spring.
      [Book II. Cent xi. page 149].

18. *Cuthbert receiving the ' Communion' received ' the cup'* [on his death-bed].

His voyage[1] steep the easier to climbe up
Christ's bloud he drank out of Life's healthfull
    cup.

' Lest any should fondly hope to decline so frequent an instance by the novel conceit of con-
comitancy (a distinction that could not *speak*
because it was not *born* in that age) it is punc-
tually stated that he distinctly received the
cup.'
      [Book II. Cent. xi. page 150].

19. *Against Marriage:* ' Amongst all the
foul mouthes belibelling marriage, one rayling
rythmer of Anselme's age, bore away the bell

---

[1] = 'Journey' whether by land or sea: G. Glossary to
my Sibbes, *s.v.*—G.

(drinking surely of Styx instead of Helicon) and
I am confident my translation is good enough
for his bald verses—

O ye that ill live, attention give, unto my fol-
    lowing rhythmes ;
Your wives, those dear mates, whom the higher
    power hates, see that ye leave them betimes.
Leave them for His sake, who a conquest did
    make, and a crown and a cross did acquire,
If any say no, I give them to know, they must
    all unto hell for their hire.
The Spouse of Christ forbids that priest his
    ministerial function
Because he did part with Christ in his heart, at
    his marriage-conjunction.
We count them all mad (if any so bad) as daring
    herein to contest;
Nor is it of spight, that this I indite, but out of
    pure love, I protest.
    [Book III. Cent. xii. page 22].

21. *On a-Beckett's ' martyrdom.'*

For Christ his Spouse, in Christ's Church, at the
    tide
Of Christ his birth, Christ his true lover dy'd.

Who dies? a priest. Why? For's flock. How?
     By th' sword.
When? At Christ's birth. Where? Altar of the
     Lord.

'Here I understand not, how properly it can be
said that Becket died *pro grege*, for his flock.
Hee did not die for feeding his flock, for any
fundamental point of religion, or for defending
his flock against the wolfe of any dangerous
doctrine : but meerly he died for his flock :
namely, that the sheep thereof (though ever so
scabb'd) might not be dress'd with tarr, and other
proper (but sharpe and smarting) medicines. I
mean that the clergie might not be punished by
the secular power, for their criminal enormities.'

        [Book III. Cent. xii. page 35].

     21. *On Henry II.*

He whom alive the world would scarce suffice
When dead, in eight foot earth contented lies.

        [Book III. Cent. xii. page 40].

     22. *Hugh Nevil :* 'Being one of the king's
special familiars, slew a lion in the Holy Land,
first driving an arrow into his breast and then

running him through with his sword, on whom
this verse was made'

Viribus Hugonis vires periêre ⎱ The strength of Hugh
Leonis.   ⎰   A lion slew.

[Book III. Cent. xii. page 41].

23. *On Richard 'the Lion-hearted :* 'I finde
two epitaphs made upon him, the first (better
for the conceit then the poetry thereof) thus
concludeth

Three places thus are sharers of his fall
Too little, one, for such a funeral.

The second may pass for a good piece of poetry
in that age.

Richard thou liest here, but were Death afraid
Of any armes, thy armes had Death dismaid.

The Latin merits Fuller's praise.

Hic, Richarde, jaces; sed Mors, si cederet, armis
Victa timore tui, cederet ipsa tuis.

[Book III. Cent. xii. page 46].

24. '*Learned Writers, Bale and Pitts.*'
'The column of learned writers I have endea-
noured to extract out of Bale and Pitts. Whereof
the later being a member of this University was
no less diligent then able to advance the honour

thereof. Let none suspect that I will enrich my
Mother by robbing my Aunt. For besides that
Cambridge is so conscientious, she will not be
accessary to my felony by receiving stolen goods:'

Tros, Tyriusque mihi nullo discrimine habetur:
  A Trojan whether he
  Or a Tyrian be
  All is the same to me.
 [Book III. Cent. xiii. page 68].

25. BACONTHORPE: ' I [FULLER] had almost over-seen John Baconthorpe being so low
in stature as but one remove from a dwarfe, of
whom one saith

 His wit was tall, in body small

Insomuch that corpus non tulisset quod ingenium
protulit, his body could not bear the books which
his brain had brought forth.'
 [Book III. Cent. xiv. page 97].

26. *William Occam :* [He] ' sided with
Lewis of Bavaria against the Pope, maintaining
the temporal power above the spiritual; he was
fain to flie to the emperor for his safety, saying
unto him

Defende me gladio et ego te defendam verbo
Defend me with thy sword and I will defend
thee with my word.

[Book III. Cent. xiv. page 98].

27. *Edward for 'protection of his native
subjects.'*

He made a statute for Lombards in this Land,
That they should in no wise take on hand
Here to inhabit, here to charge and discharge,
But forty dayes no more time had they large:
This good king by wit of such appreise
Kept his merchants and the sea from mischiefe.

[Book III. Cent. xiv. page 113].

28. *Rebellion of Wat Tyler and Jack
Straw:* 'As the Philistines [1 Samuel xiii. 17]
'came out in three companies' to destroy all the
swords and smiths in Israel : so this rabble of
rebells, making itself tripartite, endeavoured the
rooting out of all pen-knives and all appearance
of learning. One in Kent, under the aforesaid
Wat and John : the second in Suffolk ; the third
under John Littstarre a dier in Norfolke. The
former of these is described in the Latin verses
of John Gower, prince of poets in his time : of
whom we will bestow the following translation.'

Tom comes, thereat, when call'd by Wat, and
  Simm as forward we finde,
Bet calls as quick to Gibb and to Hykk, that
  neither would tarry behinde.
Gibb, a good whelp of that litter, doth help mad
  Coll more mischief to do,
And Will he doth vow, the time is come now,
  he'l joyn with their company too.
Davie complains, whiles Grigg gets the gaines,
  and Hobb with them doth partake,
Lorkin aloud, in the midst of the croud, con-
  ceiveth as deep is his stake.
Huddle doth spoil, whom Juddle doth foile, and
  Tebb lends his helping hand,
But Jack, the mad patch, men and houses[1] doth
  snatch, and kills all at his command.
[Book IV. Cent. xiv. page 139].

29. *Simon Sudbury :* ' John Gower telleth
us in his paralcl of the martyring of Simon
Sudbury, arch-bishop of Canterbury with Thomas
Becket, his predecessor '

But four conspir'd, Thomas, his blood to spill
While hundred thousands Simon help to kill.
[Book IV. Cent. xiv. page 140].

---

[1] Qu: 'horses?' the Latin however is 'domos.' G.

30. *Chaucer:* 'Our Homer: onely herein he differed

Mæonides nullas ipse reliquit opes.

Homer himself did leave no pelf,

whereas our Chaucer left behinde him a rich and worshipful estate.'
[Book IV. Cent. xiv. page 151].

31. *Chaucer:*

Of Alger Dants, Florence doth justly boast
Of Petrarch brags all the Italian coast.
England doth poet Chaucer reverence
To whom our language owes its eloquence.

'He was a great refiner and illuminer of our English tongue (and if he left it so bad, how much worse did he finde it?)'
[Book IV. Cent. xiv. page 152].

['Alger Dants' [= Dante] renders Leland's. Prædicat Algerum merito Florentia Dantem. G.]

32. 'Eton and Grammer Learning.'—'Indeed it was high time some School should be founded, considering how low grammer-learning ran then in the Land, as may appear by the following verses made for King Henry the Founder:

I

as good no doubt as the generality of that age
did afford, though (scarce deserving translation)
so, that the worst scholar in Eaton Colledg that
can make a verse can make a better '—

Devout King Henry, of that name the sixt
Born (Nic'las) on thy day, this building fixt.
In Eaton having plac'd a stone anointed
In sign, it for the clergy was appointed.
His prelates then were present, so the more
To honour the King's acts, and holy chore.
From Eastern midst, whereof just fourteen feet
If any measure, they this stone shall meet ;
Our holy James, his day, the sacred hand
Of royal Henry caus'd this stone to stand.

M. four C.'s, fourty six, since Christ was born
When H. the crown twenty-five years had
    worn.
        [Book IV. Cent. xv. page 183].

    33. *Retribution :*
Most just it is that they bad laws who make
Should themselves first of their own laws
    partake.

'Thus those who break down the banks and let
in the stream of arbitrary power (be it into the

hands of prince or people) are commonly the
first themselves which without pity are drowned
in the deluge thereof.'
[Book V. Cent. xvi. page 234].

34. *The Jesuits:* 'They had two most
antient and flourishing convents beyond the
seas; Nola in Italy as I take it, where their
home it seems gives a *bow* for their armes, and
La-Fletcha in France, where they have an *arrow*
for their device: whereupon a satyrical wit thus
guirded at them: and I hope I shall not be con-
demned as accessary to his virulency, if onely
plainly translating the same.'

Nola to them did give a Bow
La-Fletch an Arrow bring:
But who upon them will bestow
(What they deserve)—a string?
[Book VI. page 279].

35. *Feasts of Ely Abbey.*

When other Feasts before have been
If those of Elie last be seen,
'Tis like to one who hath seen night
And then beholds the day so bright.
[Book VI. page 299].

26. *Bells:* 'Such frequent firing of Abbey-Churches by lightning, confuteth the proud motto commonly written on the bells in their steeples, wherein each bell intituled itself to a sixfold efficacie :'

1. Funera plango — { Men's deaths I tell
{ By doleful knell.

2. Fulgura }
Fulmina } frango — { Lightning and thunder
{ I break asunder.

3. Sabbata frango ; — { On Sabbath, all
{ To Church I call.

4. Excito lentos · — { The sleepy head
{ I raise from bed.

5. Dissipo ventos. — { The winds so fierce
{ I doe disperse.

6. Paco cruentos. — { Men's cruell rage
{ I doe assuage.

[Book VI. page 301].   [Might have been a first (faint) sketch of Poe's memorable ' Bells.' G.]

37. *Marshes of Mantua* [Virgil].

There is no trusting to the found'ring bank
The ramme still dries his fleece so lately dank.
[Book VI. page 323].

38. *John Leland to Henry VIII.*

The sun shall sooner cease his shine to show
And moon deny her lamp to men below;
The rapid seas shall sooner fishless slide,
And bushes quite forget their birds to hide;
Great okes shall sooner cease to spread their
bowers
And Flora for to paint the meads with
flowers,
Than thou great King shall slip out of my
breast
My studies' gentle gale and quiet rest.
[Book VI. page 339].

39. *Against 'the Masse.'* — Of all his
[JEWELL'S] pupils, Edward Year (so I conceive
his name whom Lawrence Humphery in Jewel's
life pp. 77 calls Edvardum Annum) in this one
respect was most remarkable, who by his tutor
being seasoned with the love of the truth, made
a double copie of verses against the superstition
of the Masse, which so enraged Mr Welsh, the
Censor as I take it, of Corpus Christi Colledge,
against him, that he publikely and cruelly whipt
him, laying on one lash, for every verse he had
made, which I conceive was about eighty in all.
Part of them I have here thought fit to insert;

and blessed be God I may translate, and the reader peruse them, without any pain and perill, and not at the dear rate, whereat the Author composed them. I have the rather printed them because they proved as well prophetical as poetical, completely foretelling what afterwards came to pass.'

Accept O heavenly Father I request
    These few devotions from my humble breast :
See their's accesse, Heaven's gate open lyes,
    Then with my prayers I'll penetrate the skyes ;
Great God, who all things seest, doth all things
        sway,
    And all things giv'st, and all things tak'st
        away,
Let not the present Masse long-livèd be,
    Nor let it those beguile belong to Thee :
Thy people's eyes, keep it from blinding quite,
    Since to Thy word it is so opposite,
But send it to the Stygian Lakes below :
    From whence it's rise and source doth spring
        and flow.
The Lord, beholding from His Throne reply'd,
    Doubt not, young youth, firmly in Me
        confide.
I dy'd long since, now sit at the right hand
    Of my bless'd Father, and the world command :

My body wholy dwels in heavenly light
Of whom no earthly eye can gain a sight :
The shamelesse priests, of Me forge truthlesse
lies
And he that worships Masse, my Word
denyes :
A stiffeneck'd people for their sins did make
Me send them Masse, my Word away to take ;
But trust me, Scripture shall regain her sway
And wicked Masse in due time fade away.'
[Book VIII. Cent. xvi. page 9].

40. *Dr Hugh Price:* 'The said doctor in
scribed these following verses over the gate,
when the building of the Colledge [Jesus, Ox-
ford] was but begun :

Hugh Price this palace did to Jesus build
That a Law's doctor learned men might yield.

But an Oxford author telleth us that a satyrical
pen did under-write with wit and wagary enough,
these following verses :

Hugh hath not built it yet ; may it be said
He built it who hath scarce the ground-work laid?
[Book IX. Cent. xvi. page 97].

41. *Cox, bishop of Ely:* 'He was an excellent poet, though the verses written on his own tomb, are none of the best, and scarce worth our translating.'

Frail life farewell, welcome life without end,
Earth hides my corps, my soull doth heaven
    ascend ;
Christ's cock on earth, I chanted Christ his
    name,
Grant without end in heaven I sound the
    same.

[The 'gallus' = cock, it is presumed was intended as a play on his own name of Cox.   G.]
    [Book IX. Cent. xvi. page 111].

42. *Verses by Mary Queen of Scots* 'on a pane of glass at Buxton well.'

Buxton who dost with waters warme excell
    By me, perchance, never more seen, farewell.

' and at Fotheringhay Castle I have read written by her on a window, with a pointed diamond '

From the top of all my trust
Mishap hath laid me in the dust
[Book IX. Cent. xvi. page 181].

43. *Epitaph on 'Mr Luke Chaloner:' in* '*Dublin Colledge Chappel.'*

This tomb within it, here contains
Of Chaloner the sad remains.
By whose prayer and helping hand
This house erected here doth stand.
[Book IX. Cent. xvi. page 212].

44. *Humphrey Eli:*

Wonder not, England's dark with errours night
For loe here buried lies her sun so bright.
[Book X. Cent. xvii. page 34].

45. *Gunpowder Plot:*

Oh let that day be quite dash'd out of time
And not believ'd by the next generation:
In night of silence we'll conceal the crime,
Thereby to save the credit of our nation.
[Book X. Cent. xvii. page 38].

[FULLER has fine-spirited words on this 'hyperbolical rapture' in the context.   G.]

46. *The Brothers Rainolds:*

What war is this! when conquered both are glad
And either to have conquered other, sad.
[Book X. Cent. xvii. page 48].

[I may be allowed to refer to my Memoir of Dr John Rainolds prefixed to reprint of his Commentaries on Obadiah and Haggai.   G.].

47. *'Intended Colledge.'* — 'The untimely death of Prince Henry, our principal hope and the author of this designe' frustrated it :'

The modest Colledge blushèd to be stronger
Than was its lord : he died, it liv'd no longer.

[A rendering of

Erubuit Domino firmius esse suo.   G.]
[Book X. Cent. xvii. page 53].

48. PRINCE HENRY : 'He was generally lamented of the whole Land, both Universities publishing their verses in print : and give me leave to remember four made by Giles Fletcher of Trinity Colledge in Cambridge, on this Prince's plain grave, because wanting an inscription : and it will be honour enough to me if I can make thereof a translation :

If wise, amaz'd depart this holy grave :
Nor these new ashes ask, what names they have?
The graver, in concealing them was wise :
For who-so knows, strait melts in tears and dies.
[Book X. Cent. xvii. page 67].

49. *The famous, ' Conference.'* ' Some are of
opinion that the moderation and mutuall compli-
ance of these Divines might have produced much
good, if not interrupted, conceiving such lopping
might have saved the felling of Episcopacy. Yea
they are confident had this expedient been pur-
sued and perfected,'

Troy still had stood in power :
And king Priam's lofty tower
Had remained at this hower.

It might under God have been a means not only
to have *checkt* but *chockt* our Civil War in the
infancy thereof.'
[Book XI. Cent. xvii. page 175].

VIII. From History of University of
Cambridge.[1]

1. *Cambridge* :

Cambridge devoted to the Muses nine
By learned Henries piety doth shine
With learned men, which languages refine.
[Page 2].

---

[1] See 'History of the University of Cambridge since the
Conquest. 1655' folio.

2. *Humphrey Necton* :

Above the skies let's Humphrey Necton praise :
For on him, first, Cambridge, confer'd the bayes :
' that is, made him Doctor in Divinity' [Page 20].

3. *Henry and Charles Brandon, Dukes of Suffolk :* ' They were much bemoaned, the University printing a book on their funeralls, amongst which these following of Dr Parkhurst's, afterwards Bishop of Norwich, I shall endeavour to translate.'

Castor and Pollux, brothers pair
Breathing first Amicle's air,
Did with Death so bargaine make
By exchange their turns to take.
If that Death surprized one brother,
Still alive should be the other.
So the bargain was contriv'd
Both dy'd, both by turns surviv'd.
Why is fate more cruel grown
Than she formerly was known ?
Wee of brothers had a brace
Like to which did never grace
This our English earth before,
Nor the like shall grace it more.
Both bright stars, and both did stand
Hopefull bulwarks of the Land.

Both, alas! together slain
Death at once did murther twaine.
Nothing could their vertues move
Nor King Edward's hearty love.
Nor that best of mother's mones
Nor all Britaine's heavy grones.
Nothing could stern Death abate;
Oh cruel, over-cruel fate! [Page 128].
[Charles died within 'twelve hours, of the same
disease' with Henry. G].

IX. From Pisgah-Sight of Palestine.[1]

(*a*) From the letter-press.

1. *Wine of Palestine :* ' Nor were their grapes
less good than great, as a poet [Sidonius]—the
most competent judge of the matter in hand—
doth bear witness,'

I have no Gaza, Chios, Falern wine
Nor any flowing from Sarepta's vine.

---

[1] ' A Pisgah-Sight of Palestine and the Confines thereof:
with the History of the Old and New Testament acted
thereon. By Thomas Fuller B.D. London 1662' folio.

⁎ It has escaped all his Biographers, that Fuller—like
Samuel Ward—was also a designer and engraver (or etcher)
as ' T. Fuller, *fecit,*' shows, in some of the illustrations of
this volume. See specially, the spirited series, Book 4. c.
vi. page 97. G.

Thus making a quadripartite division of good wine, two members thereof, that of Gaza and Sarepta, the one fals in the tribe of Simeon, the other of Asher, both in the country of Palestine.' [Page 10].

2. *Libanus' Yews:* 'The poet [Virgil] takes notice of the plenty of yew in this province

Yew which in Ituria grows
Is neatly bended into bows.

Hence their inhabitants became excellent archers : and pity it was that their arrows were so often shot at a wrong mark—to kill and rob passengers in their journey.' [Page 104].

3. *Dagon :*

Upwards man-like he ascended
Downwards like a fish he ended.
[Page 220].

4. *Semiramis and the doves:* 'Near to this city [Askelon] there was a lake, by which Semiramis is said to be born, there fed and relieved by doves. Hence the poet Tibullus 'Alba Palestino sancta columba Syro.'

The milk-white dove esteemed divine
By Syrians of Palestine. [Page 235].

5. *Levite's concubine:* [Judges xix.] ' Oh ! the justice of Divine proceedings ! She had formerly been false to her husband ' Culpa libido fuit, pœna libido fuit.'

By lust she sinnèd and 'twas just
She should be punshèd by lust. [Page 257].

6. *Sepulchres:* The 'heathen used in like manner to interr their dead in high-ways : yea their sepulchres served to measure the distances of places' [Virgil Ecl : 9].

Hence ev'n mid-way it is for us : for near,
Bianor's tomb beginneth to appear. [Page 298].

7. *Tabernacle and Temple:*

Their faces neither diverse nor the same
But such as sisters very well became.

'The latter being none other than the imitation of the former with proportionable addition : as indeed what is the Tabernacle of Grace but the Temple of Glory contracted or the Temple of Glory but the Tabernacle of Grace dilated' [Page 358].

8. *Giants: Diomedes and Aeneas: Aeneas and Turnus:*

A stone he snatch'd and threw, a stone indeed
So huge, so heavy, two men now had need
To heave it up, such dwarfs our days do breed.—
[Page 363].

9. *Horses in sacrifice to the sun:* ' The Persians offered horses unto the Sun and Ovid renders some reason thereof'

Horses to the beamèd sun's the Persian's gift :
Slow sacrifice ill fits a God so swift. [Page 386].

10. *Dew* [Genesis xxvii. 39.] ' Behold thy dwelling shall be the fatness of the earth, and of the dew of heaven from above.' Earth is by Isaac first mentioned because by Esau most minded. But oh the difference betwixt the dew of heaven in Jacob's and Esau's blessing! [Genesis xxvii. 28]. In the former it signified God's favour with an undoubted right unto and sanctified use of, Divine promises, service and Sacraments : whereas in this blessing of Esau, heavenly dew, was in effect but earthly dew, temporall, terrestrial fertility, allowed to this mountainous land of Edom, whose lean hills were larded with

many fruitful vallies interposed. Heathen authors confess [Statius]

Whatever noble worth destils
On Pontus nut-trees, or what fils
The fruitful Idumean hils.
[Page 30 : Book IV. c. 2.]

11. *Egypt.*

A Land content with home-bred ware
For foreign wealth she doth not care,
Or whether heavens do frown or smile,
Her confidence is all in Nile.
[Lucan *l.* 8]. [Page 81 : Book 4. c. 5.]

12. *Mock-tears:* [Jeremiah ix. 17, 18].

Thy tears were trusted : do they falshood know?
Yea they have tricks, at will they come and go.
[Ovid.]

' But as parents when their children cry for *nothing,* use to beat them that they might cry for *something:* so God threatned that the miseries of Jerusalem should afterwards turn their faigned and strained wailings into sound and sincere sorrow : when those tears — formerly but the adopted children—should become the natural issue of their heavy hearts.' [Page 118. Book 4. c. 6.]

K

13. *Idols:* 'In all ages some were found who flouted at such superstitions: amongst these the poet brings in an idol thus speaking,'

Time out of minde a fig-tree stock I grew,
An useless block, before the workmen knew
Benches or gods to make me—smal the ods—
Resolv'd at last of me to make his gods.
[Page 126. Book 4 c. 7.]

14. *Idol-calf:* [Virgil].

My calfe I lay—lest you mislike't, both tides
She comes to th' pale [pail] and suckles twain
besides. [Page 129: Book 4 c. 7.]

(*b*) From the Maps.

(1) Engraved title-page 1650:
Votum Authoris
Terrestres Solymas mihi qui scripsisse dedisti,
Cœlestes tandem des habitare, Devs.

Dicat. T. F.

(2) From General Map of Palestine—1650.

Virjo amplissimo
Duô Guilielmo Paston, Equiti aureato
disjunctissimoerum regionum Αὐ7όπλῃ
Omnia perlustra quæ profert chartula lapsus
Condona erranti recta tuere precor
Nam tibi Judæa est, tibi tam sunt ostia nili
Quam tua mendicis hospita nota domus.

(3) Map of Jerusalem—1650 pp. 308.

> Eduardo Montagu
> Armigero, inter Juvenes
> doctos noblissimo nobiles
> doctissimo (quasi posthabi
> ta natalium claritate se
> totum litteris destinasset)
> filio
> Honoratissimi Eduardi
> Baronis Montagu, qui
> me languidum, exulem, nullum
> primus fouit, hospitio exce-
> pit, munificentia recreauit
> quin et
> quod omnium caput
> est, filiolum meum
> (senectutis meae spem
> vnicam) libere insti-
> tuendum curauit.
> Hierosolymarum
> Typum dedico.   T. F.[1]

(4) Fragmenta Sacra :—1650 B. v. p. 202.
Nobilissimis viris Johanni et Eduardo
Russello, Francisi nuper Comitis Bedfordiae
filiis natu minoribus.

---

[1] This is not given as verse, but as illustrating 'liaiuous
Sinne,' etc. dedication.   G.

Fragmenta hæc vestri ne dedignentur Honores
Sint Fragmenta licet, sunt ea Sacra tamen.
Mensuræ Ebrœæ, priscæ numismata Formæ.
Vestis Aaronis Mystica, quanta tegens!
Destructi (ah miserum) Templi captiva supellex
Roma triumphatrix, Cæsareumque Decus.
Sic lacera in nimios Tabula est divisa locellos,
Integer ad vester Totus et Author erit.

X. From 'the Holy Warre'[1]

1. *Issues:*

May he never speed
Who from the issue censures of the deed.

---

[1] 'The Historie of the Holy Warre: By Thomas Fuller,
B.D. . . . Cambridge 1651' folio. By the kindness of
its possessor—Mr Winters, Church-yard, Waltham Abbey,—
the following MS. lines written in a copy of the 'Holy
Warre' by some contemporary and admirer of our Worthy,
are herewith subjoined: more accurately than as given in
Notes and Queries [3d Series: 2d half 1867 p. 226]. Who
was R. H.? G.

ON THE TITLE AND AUTHOR;

Shall warr, the ofspring of rebellious pryde
disturber of heuens peace, be glorifyed
with a sacred epithite? tis a iarr,
that it should haue the tearme of Holy warr;
It is not surely meant the very thing
is holy, but the holy cause doth bring

'Though an argument fetch't from the successe is but a cyphre in itself yet it increaseth
a number when joyned with others.'
[Page 16 :B. i. c. 10.]

2. *Baldwine:* 'For the rest we referre the
reader to the dull epitaph written on his tombe,
which (like the verses of that age) runneth in a
kind of rhythme, though it can scarce stand on
true feet :'

Baldwine another Maccabee for might
Hope, help of State, of Church, and both's
    delight :
Cedar, with Egypt's Dan of him afraid,
Bloudy Damascus to him tribute paid :
    Alas ! here in this tombe is laid.
[Page 62 : B. II. c. 13.]

---

a holy stile to a destructiue game ;
A Turk may haue an honorable name :
Yet warr is not unlawfull, though it kill ;
the Circumstance doth make it good or ill ;
But howso'er the cause or matter bee,
thy pithie lynes, and witt doe render thee
let pryde and envie strugle what they can,
Fuller, the holy, wise, and learned man.
         R: H:

3.† *Alexius the Grecian emperour:* 'We had almost forgotten what happened in this yeare— the death of Alexius, the Grecian emperour, that arch-hypocrite and grand enemie of this warre. On whom we may bestow this epitaph :

If he of men the best doth know to live
Who best knows to dissemble, justly then
To thee, Alexius, we this praise must give,
That thou to live didst know the best of men.
    And this was it at last did stop thy breath
    Thou knew'st not how to counterfeit with
    Death. [Page 64 : B. II. c. 14.]

4. *Lamentable death of King Fulk :* 'He was slain in earnest as following his sport in hunting, to the great grief of his subjects. And we may heare him thus speaking his epitaph :

A hare I hunted, and Death hunted me ;
The more my speed was, was the worse my
    speed :
For as well-mounted I away did flee,
Death caught and kill'd me, falling from my
    steed.
    Yet this mishap an happie misse I count
    That fell from horse that I to heaven might
    mount. [Page 74 : B. ii. c. 23.]

5. *Frederick, the worthy emperour :* ' We may heare his sorrowful army speaking thus his epitaph unto him'

Earth scarce did yeeld ground enough for thy
    sword
To conquer : how then could a brook afford
Water to drown thee ? brook, which some doth
    fear
(O guilty conscience !) in a map t' appear.
Yet blame we not the brook, but rather think
The weight of our own sinnes did make thee
    sink.
Now sith 'tis so, wee'l fetch a brackish main
Out of our eyes, and drown thee once again.
      [Page 116 : B. III. c. 4.]

6.† *Conrade :* ' This may serve for his epitaph

The crown I never did enjoy alone ;
Of half a kingdome I was half a king.
Scarce was I on when I was off the throne ;
Slain by two slaves, me basely murdering.
  And thus the best man's life at mercie lies
  Of vilest varlets that their own despise.
      [Page 125 : B. III. c. 10.]

7. *King Guy:* ' We then dismisse King Guy,
hearing him thus taking his farewell '

I steer'd a State warre-tost against my will:
Blame then the storm, not th' pilot's want of
    skill,
That I the kingdome lost, whose empty
    style
I sold to England's king for Cyprus isle.
I pass'd away the Land I could not hold ;
Good ground I bought, but only aire I sold.
    Then as a happy merchant may I sing
    Though I must sigh as an unhappy king.
       [Page 126 : B. III. c. 10.]

8. ' *King Richard taken prisoner in Austria :*
sold and sent to the emperour: dearly ransomed,
returneth home '—' After this money, Peter of
Bloys (who had drunk as deep of Helicon as any
of that age) sendeth this good prayer: making an
apostrophe to the emperour or to the Duke of
Austria or to both together'

    And now, thou basest avarice
      Drink till thy belly burst,
   Whil'st England poures large silver
      showres
    To satiate thy thirst.

And this we pray, Thy money may
And thou be like accurst.
[Page 131 : B. III. c. 13.]

9. *French-rhyme: Crusades.*

Jesus Lord ! repair our losse ;
Restore to us thy holy crosse.
[Page 152 : B. III. c. 24.]

10. '*The pastorells killed in France:*' 'A
rhymer of that age (or in courtesie call him a
poet,) made this epitaph on them :

Learn to put together well
What M. C. C. L. I. do spell ;
When some devilish fiend in France
Did teach the Shepherds how to dance.
[Page 206 : B. IV. c. 21.]

XI. From 'the Holy State'[1]

1. *The Elder Brother:* 'He rather desires his
father's life than his living. This was one of the
principal reasons (but God knows how true) why

---

[1] 'The Holy State. By Thomas Fuller B.D. and Pre-
bendary of Sarum. 4° edn. London, 1663' folio.

Philip the second, king of Spain, caused in the
year 1568, Charles, his eldest son to be executed
for plotting his father's death, as was pretended.
And a wit [Opmerus (?)] in such difficult toyes
accommodated the numeral letters in Ovid's verse
to the year wherein the Prince suffered.

FILIVS ante DIeM patrios InqVIrIt In annos
1568.

Before the tIMe the oVer-hasty sonne
Seeks forth hoVV near the father's LIfe Is Done.
[B. I. c. 14. page 41.]
1568.

2. *The younger brother:* 'To use the herald's
language, he may say'

This to my elder brother I must yield
I have the *charge* but he hath all the field.
[B. I. c. 15. p. 42.]

3. *Julius Scaliger:* 'His skill in physick was
as great as his practice therein was happy : in so
much that he did many strange and admirable
cures.   Hear how a noble and learned pen
[Stephanus Boetius] doth commend him'

On snowy Caucasus there grew no root
Of secret power, but he was privy to't :

On cold Riphean hills no simple grew,
But he the force thereof and virtue knew :
Wherewith—apply'd by his successful art—
Such sullen souls as would this world depart,
He forc't still in their bodies to remain
And from death's door fetch'd others back again.
[B. II. c. 8 page 71.]

4. *The faithful minister:* ' He counts the success of his ministry the greatest. preferment. Yet herein God hath humbled many painful pastours, in making them to be clouds, to rain not over Arabia the happy but over the stony or desert : so that they may complain with the herdsman in the poet

My starveling bull
Ah ! woe is me !
In pasture full
How lean is he !
[B. II. c. 9 page 77.]

5. *William Perkins:* ' He was of a ruddy complexion, very fat and corpulent, lame of his right hand : and yet this Ehud with a left-handed pen did shake the Romish cause and as one [Holland] saith

Though nature thee of thy right hand bereft
Right well thou writest with the hand that's
left.

[The Latin may interest :
Dextera quantumvis fuerat tibi manca, docendi
Pollebas mira dexteritate tamen. G.]
[B. II. c. 11. page 84.]

6. *Simony:* 'We confess it a personal vice
amongst us, but not to be charged as a Church-
sin : which by penal laws it doth both prohibit
and punish. Did Rome herein look upon the
dust behind her own doors, she would have but
little cause to call her neighbour slut. What
saith the epigram ?

That *Peter* was at Rome, there's strife about it
That *Simon* was there, none ever did doubt it.

[The Latin is as follows :

An Petrus fuerat Romæ, sub judice lis est
Simonem Romæ nemo fuisse negat. G.]
[B. II. c. 12. page 88.]

7. *The good patron :* 'Afterwards, to invite
lay-men to build and endow Churches, the Bishops

departed with their right, to the lay-patrons, according to the verse

A patron's he that did endow with lands
Or built the Church or on whose ground it
    stands.

it being conceived reasonable that he who paid the Churche's portion should have the main stroke in providing her an husband.' [B. II. c. 12. page 87.]

8. *Hope disappointed:* 'Daily experience tenders too many examples. A gentleman who gave a *basilisk* for his arms or crest, promised to make a young kinsman of his, his heir, which kinsman to ingratiate himself painted a basilisk in his study and beneath it these verses'

Falleris aspectu basiliscum occidere, Plini
Nam vitæ nostræ spem basiliscus alit

The basilisk's the onely stay
My life preserving still ;
Pliny, thou li'dst when thou didst say
The basilisk doth kill.

But this rich gentleman dying, frustrated his ex-

pectation and bequeathed all his estate to another.
whereupon the epigram was thus altered.

Certe aluit, sed spe vana, spes vana venenum :
Ignoscas, Plini, verus es historicvs.
Indeed vain hopes to me he gave,
Whence I my poison drew :
Pliny, thy pardon now I crave
Thy writings are too true.

[B. III. c. 9. page 161.]

9. *Tombes:* ''Tis a provident way to make
one's tombe in one's lifetime, both hereby to prevent the negligence of heirs and to mind him of
his mortality. Virgil tells us that when bees
swarm in the aire and two armies meeting together, fight as it were a set battel with great
violence, cast but a little dust upon them and they
will be quiet.'

These stirrings of their minds, and strivings vast
If but a little dust on them be cast
Are straitwayes stinted and quite over-past.

Thus the most ambitious motions and thoughts
of man's mind are quickly quell'd when dust is
thrown on him, whereof his fore-prepared sepul-
chre is an excellent remembrancer.

[B. III. c. 14. page 175.]

10. *The same:* ' Thus love if not to the dead, to the living, will make him if not a grave, a hole: and it was the begger's epitaph *Nudus eram vivus, mortuus ecce tegor.*

Naked I liv'd, but being dead
Now behold I'am coverèd.
[B. III. c. 14. page 177.]

11.† *Finis:* ' When one had set out a witless pamphlet, writing *Finis* at the end thereof, another wittily wrote beneath it

—— Nay there thou li'st my friend
In writing foolish books there is no end.
[B. III. c. 18. page 187.]

[The ' another' was doubtless Fuller himself. G.].

12. *Moderation:*

Both ends o' th' table furnish'd are with meat
Whilst they in middle nothing had to eat.
They were none of the wisest well I wist
Who made bliss in the middle to consist.
[B. III. c. 20. page 202.]

13. *Gravitie:* 'That may be done privately
without breach of gravity, which may not be done
publickly. As when a father makes himself his
child's rattle, sporting with him till the father
hath devoured the wise man in him, *Equitans in
arundine longa.*

Instead of stately steed
Riding upon a reed.
[B. III. c. 21 page 205.]

14. ' *Grand' Churches:*

The Church did blush more glory for to have
Then had her Lord. He begg'd : should she be
brave.   [B. III. c. 24. page 217.]

15. *The good Bishop:* 'In his grave writings
he aims at God's glory and the Church's peace,
with that worthy prelate, the second Jewel of
Salisbury, whose comments and controversies will
transmit his memory to all posterity :

Whose dying pen did write of *Christian
Union*
How Church with Church might safely keep
Communion.
Commend his care, although the cure do misse :
The woe is ours, the happinesse is his :

Who finding discords daily to encrease
Because he could not live would dy, in peace.
[B. IV. c. 9. page 270.]

[Davenant is referred to : his mother was sister of
Fuller's. G.].

16. *Augustine:* 'His diet was very cleanly
and sparing, yet hospitable in the entertaining of
others : and had this distich wrote on his table'

He that doth love an absent friend to jeer
May hence depart, no room is for him here.
[B. IV. c. 10. page 275.]

17. *Ridley and Hooper:* 'In like manner,
not much before, his [Ridley] dear friend, Master
Hooper suffered with great torment : the wind
(which too often is the bellows of great fires)
blowing it away from him once or twice. Of all
the martyrs in those days, these two endured most
pain, it being true that each of them *querebat in
ignibus ignes :'*

And still he did desire
For fire in midd'st of fire

both desiring to burn and yet both their upper
parts were but confessours when their lower parts
were martyrs and burnt to ashes.'
[B. IV. c. 11. page 283.]

18. *Lady Jane Grey*:

What eyes thou readst with Reader, know I not:
Mine were not dry when I this story wrote.
[B. IV. c. 14. page 298.]

19. *Queen Elizabeth and the Spanish Em-*
bassadour: ' Nor was her poetick vein less happy
in Latine. When a little before the Spanish inva-
sion in '88, the Spanish embassadour (after a
larger representation in his master's demands) had
summed up the effect thereof in a tetrastitch, who
instantly in one verse rejoyned her answer. We
will presume to English both, though confessing
the Latine loseth lustre by the translation.'

.

These to you are our commands,
Send no help to th' Netherlands :
Of the treasure took by Drake
Restitution you must make :
And those abbies built anew
Which your father overthrew :
If for any peace you hope
In all points restore the Pope.

The Queen's extempore return :
Ad Grecas, bone rex, fiant mandata calendas
   Worthy king, know this your will
   At latter Lammas wee'l fulfil.
           [B. IV. c. 15. page 303.]

    20. *Gustavus Adolphus:* 'I find a most
learned pen [Hakewill] apply these Latin verses
to this noble prince : and it is honour enough
for us to translate them'

More then a Priest he in the Church might
   pass.
More then a Prince in Commonwealth he was.
More then a Counseller in points of State.
More then a Lawyer matters to bebate.
More then a General to command outright.
More then a Souldier to perform a fight.
More then a man to bear affliction strong.
More then a man good to forgive a wrong.
More then a Patriot countrey to defend.
True friendship to maintain, more then a
   Friend.
More then familiar sweetly to converse.
And though in sports more then a lion fierce;
To hunt and kill the game ; yet be exprest
More then Philosopher in all the rest.
        [B. IV. c. 18. page 321.]

21. *Heir-apparent:*

His worth above his wealth appears
And vertues go beyond his years.
[B. IV. c. 19. page 322.]

XI. From the Profane State. [1]

1. *The harlot :* 'Besides by many wicked
devices she seeks on purpose to make herself
barren' . . .

Which wicked projects first from hell did flow,
And thither let the same in silence go,
Best known of them who did them never know.
[B. V. c. 1. page 345.]

2. *Joan of Arc:*

Cruelty to a woman
Brings honour unto no man.

'We will close the different opinions which
several Authours had of her, with this epitaph :'

Here lies Joan of Arc, the which
Some count saint and some count witch;

---

[1] 'The Profane State.   By Thomas Fuller B.D. and Pre-
bendary of Sarum.   London 1663.' folio.

Some count man and something more ;
Some count maid and some a whore ;
Her life's in question, wrong or right:
Her death's in doubt, by laws or might
Oh innocence take heed of it
How thou too near to guilt dost sit.
(Meantime France a wonder said
A woman rule 'gainst Salique law)
But, reader, be content to stay
Thy censure till the Judgment-day :
Then shalt thou know and not before
Whether saint, witch, man, maid or whore.
[B. V. c. 5. pp. 363, 364.]

3. *Atheist :*

On earth were atheists many
In hell there is not any.
[B. v. c. 7. page 368.]

4. *Jehu :*

Three weaklings we, a wife for war too mild
Laertes old, Telemachus a child.

So thrice a year should Jehu onely be king
over such an impotent company of old men,
women and children.' [B. V c. 9. page 377.]

5. † *Abolition of Universities:*

Which we believe and wish may then be done
When all blear eyes have quite put out the sun.
[B. V. c. 11. page 387.] [1]

6. *The Liar:*

When Jesuits unto us answer, Nay
They do not English speak, 'tis Greek they say.
[B. V. c. 12. page 390.]

XII. From 'Abel Redevivus.' [2]

1. BERENGARIUS : [of Tours : Born (probably

---

[1] Fuller's authority for his preposterous accusation in the
context, of Greenwood and Barrow is 'Dr Soame's writing
against them: lib. 2. page 4. But as against Soames see
'A True Relation of Two Merchants of London, who were
taken Prisoners by the Cavaliers, and of the barbarous
cruelty inflicted on them: together with the great familiarity
of Dr Soames, Vicar of Staynes with the Cavaliers and
of their familiarities with his daughters 1642. [4°]. G.

[2] 'Abel Redevivus [*sic*]: or the Dead yet Speaking. The
Lives and Deaths of the modern Divines: written by several
able and learned men..........1651' [4°] Fuller names Berengarius, Huss, Jerome, Cranmer, Fox, Junius and Perkins as
by himself, and adds ' etc.' The 'most part of the poetry' he
assigns to Master Quarles, father and son: but I understand
this to exclude the 'Lines' in his own Lives. 'Abel Redevivus ' has been re-printed under the supervision of ' William
Nichols' for Tegg: *modernized* but very fairly if rather pe-
dantically edited. 2 vols. cr. 8° 1867. G.

in 1020) Died January 6th 1088. G.] ' We leave
him to stand or fall to his owne Master, according
to that concluding disticke, which we find in an
author :'

Cùm nihil ipse vides propriâ quin labe laboret
  Tu tua fac cures, cætera mitte Deo.

'Seeing nought thou seest but faults are in the best
Looke thou unto thyselfe, leave God the rest.'
[Pp. 7, 8.]

Most worthily may this Divine
Old Berengarius, fairely shine
Within this skie of lustrious starres
Who 'gainst Rome's errorours fought Truth's warres:
Confuting, with high approbation
Rome's figment, Transubstantiation ;
Which did that hierarchie so vex
And with such passion so perplex
That they would never give him rest
But did his soule so much molest,
That at the last, by fraud and force
They made him—with most sad remorse
Two several times his cause recant ;
Him of his crown thus to supplant.
Thus, O, thus, oft, Sol's rayes most rare
With duskie clouds eeclipsèd are.

2. John Huss: [Reformer and Martyr:
Born 1376 (?): Died July 7th 1415.   G.]

This most illustrious lamp of Gospel light
Which in Bohemia first shon forth most bright
By this renownèd martyres industry,—
Heavenly, heroick Huss, yet furiously
Affronted was by Papall enemies.
But in the midst of this their rage, did rise
Among themselves, a mighty schisme and rent
Three anti-popes at once : by which event
Renownèd Huss did great advantage gain,
The Gospel's light to propagate, maintain.
But, at the last, that schism being sew'd-up
Againe they fill their wrath's and rage's cup ;
And gave it Huss to drink, who valiantly
Drank-up the same, to death's extremity :
And though they painted-devils placed on his
        head [1]
Yet he their scorn and rage did nothing dread.
Thus, faithlesse Rome, breaking her promise given.
In fiery-chariot sent his soul to heaven.

[Page 20.]

---

[1] 'A paper, whereon devils were anticly [= grotesquely]
painted, was put upon him; he wearing those shadows
on his head, whose substance his enemies felt in their
heart.' F.

3. JEROME OF PRAGUE : [Reformer and Martyr: Born 1378 (?) : Died May 30th 1416. G.]

This brave Bohemian worthy may, indeed
His brother Huss most worthily succeed ;
And, as two twins, for their heroic spirit,
The one the other's honour may inherit.
For by John Huss, Jerome was blestly ayded,
Where by the Romish-rout he was invaded :
And Jerome, hearing Huss was wrong'd by Rome
To vindicate his quarrell did presume ;
But, in the tryal, found his heeles tript up
Fearfull (by Romish rage) to taste his cup.
Yet, at the last, that tempting blast ore blown
His doubled and redoubled zeal was shown ;
Stoutly recanting his forced recantation,
To th' death he hated Rome's abomination.
Which did their Romish furie so inflame,
That, torturing him, they tygers fierce became :
His head (like Huss) with painted divels array'd
His soule to heaven outrageous flames convay'd.
[Page 30.]

4. CRANMER [Reformer and Martyr: Born
1489 : Died March 21, 1556. G.]

'Twas not inticing honour could remove
The constant heart of Cranmer from the love
Of sound divinity ; he alwayes stood

Firme to God's cause, and dy'd it with his blood.
A true seraphicke and tyrannicke fire
Proved—as it were—ambitious to aspire :
And both prevail'd, being willing to controule ;
Th' one burnt his body, th' other cured his soule.
Image-adoring Papists, boast your fils ;
Ye sent a soul to heaven against your wils.
What can ye say, but this,—your rage was spent ;
Ye did him good, though with an ill intent ?
Pricke up your cares and heare this fatall tone,
Those fires which made him screek, will make
     you gron.   [Page 228.]

     5. JOHN Fox or FOXE [' Martyrologist :' Born
1517 : Died April 18, 1587.   G.]

Rare Fox (well furr'd with patience) liv'd a life
In's youthfull age devoted unto strife ;
For the blind Papists of those frantick times
Esteem'd his virtues as his greatest crimes.
The hot persuit of their ful crying hounds
Forced him to flye beyond the lawlesse bounds :
Of their hot-sented malice : though their skill
Was great in hunting, yet our Fox was still
Too crafty for them : though they ranged about
From place to place, they could not finde him out :
And when they saw their plots could not prevaile
To bless their noses with his whisking taile,
They howl'd out curses, but could not obtain ;

Their prey being fled, their curses proved in vaine:
From whence I think this proverb came at first,—
' Most thrives the Fox that most of all is curst.'
[Page 383.]

6. Fr. Junius [French Protestant: Born
1545: Died Oct. 13, 1602. G.]

Reader, observe, and thou shalt finde
A rare and well-reformèd minde :
He that in his youthfull dayes
Scorch'd his conscience by the blaze
Of wanton fires, refused at last
The heat of an atheisticke blast ;
He started from the deep abyss
Of vilenesse to the height of bliss ;
And then that light which fil'd his breast
Gave himselfe and others rest ;
That they which did before contemne
His deeds, imbraced him as a jem ;
And thought him fitting to be set
Within the Church's cabonet,
His vertue pay'd what vice had scoared
And age abhor'd what youth adored.
[Page 450.]

7. WILLIAM PERKINS [Divine : Born 1558 :
Died 1602.   G.]

Of all the worthies in this learned role,
Our English Perkins may, without controle,
Challenge a crowne of bayes to deck his head
And second unto none be numberèd,
For's learning, wit and worthy parts divine,
Wherein his fame resplendently did shine
Abroad and eke at home, for's preaching rare
And learned writings almost past compare ;
Which were so high esteem'd, that some of them
Translated were (as a most precious jem)
Into the Latine, French, Dutch, Spanish tongue,
And rarely valued both of old and young.
And (which was very rare) them all did write
With his left hand, his right being useless quite :
Borne in the first, dying in the last, year
Of Queen Eliza, a princesse without peer.
[Page 440.]

XIV. From ' Mixt Contemplations on These
Times' and ' Personal Meditations :' in all the
collected editions of ' Good Thoughts,' etc.

1. *All for the present :* ' Oh ! give me that
good man's gracious temper who earnestly desired
the prosperity of the Church, whatsoever became

of himself, whose verses I will offer to translate.'

Buried in earth or drown'd in th' main
Eat up by worms or fishes:
I pray the pious may obtain
For happy times, their wishes.
[M. C. XXII.]

2. *Niniveh:* 'But what is now become of Niniveh? It is even buried in its own ruins and may have this epitaph upon it:'

Hic jacet finis infiniti
Here lieth the *end* of what was *endless*.
[*Ibid.* XXIX.]

3. *Good augury:* 'I was much affected with reading that distick in Ovid, as having somewhat extraordinary therein:'

Tarpeia quondam predixit ab ilice cornix
Est, bene non potint dicere, dixit, erit.
The crow sometimes did sit and *spell* [1]

On top of Tarpie-hall;
She could not say *all's well, all's well*
But said *it shall, it shall*

---

[1] To fore-tell; hence spelman. F.

'But what do I listen to the language of the crow, whose black colours hath a cast of hell therein, in superstitious soothsaying. Let us hearken to what the dove of the Holy Spirit saith.'

[M. C. XXXV.]

4. *Ovid's line:*

Father an me pity take
Verses I no more will make.   (P. M. XI.)

XIV. From the 'Worthies.' [1]

1. *Scarlet-habit of Cardinals:* 'whereof Theodore Beza tartly enough thus expresseth himself:'

My clothes in purple liquor ne'er were stew'd,
  Nor garments (trust me) richly dy'd in grain.
Those robes you see so red, I have imbrew'd
  In gore of guiltless saints, whom I have slain.
Or, mindful of the faults they hide, with shame
The bashful clothes do blush their wearer's
      blame.   [C. IV. page 15.]

2. *Lord Chancellors:* 'I find another notation of this office, some deducing his name *a cancellando* from *cancelling* things amisse, and

---

[1] 'The History of the Worthies of England. Endeavoured by Thomas Fuller, D.D. London, 1662,' folio.

rectifying them by the rules of equity and a good
conscience : and this relateth to no meaner author
then Johannes Sarisburiensis.'

'Tis he, who cancelleth all cruel lawes,
   And in kings' mandates equity doth cause.
If aught to Land or laws, doth hurtful prove,
   The care that hurt doth speedily remove.
    [C. VI. page 16 mispaged.]

3. *Needless books :* ' Solomon was sensible of
this vanity, even in his time, when pronouncing
" of books there is no end." The heathen poet
took notice thereof, *Scribimus indocti doctique
Pœmata passim :*'
    Poems write a main we do
    Learnèd and unlearnèd too.
    [C. X. page 29.]

4. *Modern pamphleteers :* ' Here I expect that
the judicious reader will excuse me, if I take no
notice of many modern pamphleteers : seeing
unlearned scribblers are not ranked with learned
writers ; yea it was, though tartly, truly said, to
the author of such a book :'

Whilst others flow with faults, but one is past
In all thy book : 'tis fault from first to last.

' Indeed the Press, at first a virgin, then a chaste wife, is since turned common, as to prostitute herself to all scurrilous pamphlets.'

[C. X. pages 29, 30.]

5.† *Henry Keble, Lord Mayor of London,* 1511 : ' who besides other benefactions in his lifetime, re-builded Alder-Mary-Church run to very ruines, and bequeathed at his death a thousand pounds for the finishing thereof. Yet within sixty years after, his bones were unkindly yea inhumanely, cast out of the vaulte wherein they were buried, his monument plucked down for some wealthy person of the present times, to be buried therein. I could not but on this occasion rub up my old poetry : '

Facit Indignatio Versus.
The Author to Alder-Mary Church.

' Ungrateful Church, orerun with rust
Lately buried in the dust ;
Utterly thou hadst been lost,
If not preserv'd by Keble's cost :
A thousand pounds, might it not buy
Six foot in length for him to lie ?
But, ousted of his quiet tombe,
For later corps he must make roome :

Tell me where his dust is cast
Though't be late, yet now at last;
All his bones with scorne ejected,
I will see them re-collected:
Who faine myself would kinsman prove
To all that did God's temples love.

Alder-Mary Churche's Answer.

' Alas? my innocence excuse:
My Wardens they did me abuse.
Whose avarice his ashes sold
That goodness might give place to gold;
As for his reliques, all the town
They are scattered up and down;
Seest a Church repaired well?
There a sprinkling of them fell:
See'st a new Church lately built?
Thicker there his ashes spilt:
O that all the Land throughout
Keble's dust were throune about;
Places scattered with that seed
Would a crop of Churches breed.'
[C. XI. page 33.]

6. *Exhortation to deeds of charity:* ' The
best-disposed to bounty may need a remembrancer: and I am sure that nightingale which would
wake, will not be angry with the thorn which

M

pricketh her breast when she noddeth. Besides
it is a truth what the poet saith,'

Who, what thou dost, thee for to do doth move
Doth praise thy practice and thy deeds approve.
[C. XI. page 39.]

7. *Altering of surnames:* 'Hence it is that
the same name hath been so often disguised unto
the staggering of many, who have mistook them
for different: *Idem non idem, queruntque in
nomine nomen.'*

The *same* they thought was not the same ;
And in their *name* they sought their *name*.

'Thus I am informed that the honourable name
of Villiers is written in fourteen several.ways,
in their own evidence.'   [C. XVII. page 51.]
[Shakespeare, Raleigh, Sibbes, Airay, afford like
examples.   G.]

8. *Associates of a man's life :*
We by their company do own
Men by themselves to us unknown.

The Latin is
Noscitur è socio qui non noscetur ab ipso.
[C. XX. page 55.]

9. *Descents:* 'If enquiry be made into all men's descents, it would be found true what the poet doth shewe :'

The first of all thine ancestors of yore
Was but a shepheard, or——I say no more.
[C. XXV. page 74.]

10. *' Haste makes waste.'* — *Objection* to the Worthies 'prevented' [= 'anticipated.' G.] 'You have hudled your book too soon to the presse, for a subject of such a nature. You should have sent to the gentry of several counties, to have furnished you with memorables out of their own pedegrees and should have taken a longer time to compose them.'

' Eight years digest what you have rudely hinted,
And in the ninth year let the same be printed !'

Answer. ' That *ninth* year might happen eight years after my death, being sensible of the impression of age upon me; and a stranger to my method would hardly rally my scattered posthumed notes.' [C. XXV. page 74.] [The ' Worthies' did prove to be ' posthume' and the son brought it out with little of the skill or care of the father as the many blundering folio, shews. G.]

11. *Episcopacy and Presbytery: Objection:*
' In your Protestant writers you promiscuously
mingle some very zealous for Episcopacy, others
as active for Presbytery.' . . *Answer:* ' I had
rather privately bemoan than publickly proclaim
the difference betwixt them when alive : charit-
ably believing that being dead

> Now they are agreèd well
> And in bliss together dwell.'
> [C. XXV. page 74.]

12. *Living persons: Objection:* ' You have
omitted many memorable persons still surviving,
as meriting as any you have inserted. *Answer:*
The return of Martial in a case not much unlike
may much befriend me herein :'

> Deceasèd authors thou admir'st alone
> And only praisest poets dead and gone.
> Vacerra, pardon me : I will not buy
> Thy praise so dear as for the same to dye.

' All men being like-minded with Martial herein, none surviving will distaste their omission in
a work, for reasons afore alledged (save in some
cases) confined to the memories of the departed.'
[C. XXV. page 76.]

13. *Numerousness of 'writers:'* Omissions are apologized for ' for their numerousnesse and therefore I may make use of the Latine distick wherewith John Pitscus closeth his book of English writers.'

More volums to our volums must we bind ;
And when that's done, a bound we cannot find.
[C. XXVI. page 79.]

14. *Birth-place:*

A thankful man will feed
The place which did him breed.
[C. XXVI. page 80.]

15. *English ' ape' the French:*
—— It is to us a pain
This should be said and not gain-said again.
[Berkshire : Proverbs.]

16.† *Royal Children:* ' As for the other children of . . . . . . Eleanor . . . . . . viz. Henry, Alphonse, Blanche, dying in their infancy immediately after their baptism, it is enough to name them and to bestow this joynt epitaph upon them.'

Cleansèd at font we drew untainted breath
Not yet made bad by life, made good by death
[*Ibid.*]

17. *Sir John Mason:*

He saw five princes which the scepter bore
Of them was privy-councellor to four.   [*Ibid.*]

18. *Ancient gentry:*

Of names which were in days of yore
Few remain here of a great store.   [*Ibid.*]

19.† *Richard Cox and Prince Edward:* 'He
was sent for to be instructor to Prince Edward,
which, with good conscience, to his great credit,
he discharged.   Here reader forgive me in hazard-
ing thy censure, in making and translating a
distick upon them.'

Præceptor doctus, docilis magis an puer ille?
Ille puer docilis, præceptor tu quoque doctus.
Master more able, child of more docility?
Docile the child, master of great ability.
[Buckinghamshire.]

20. *Dame Hester Temple:* 'I confess very
many of her descendants dyed before her death:
in which respect she was far surpassed by a Roman
matron, on whom the poet thus epitapheth it, in
her own person:'

Twenty nine births Callicrate I told
And of both sexes saw none sent to grave?
I was an hundred and five winters old,
Yet stay from staff my hand did never crave.
[Buckinghameshire.]

21. *Baskets:* ' Martial confesseth baskets to
have been a British invention, though Rome afterwards laid claim thereunto.'

I, foreign basket, first in Brittain known
And now by Rome accounted for her own.
[Cambridgeshire.]

22. *Matthew Paris:*

Matthew, here cease thy pen in peace, and study
on no more
Nor do thou rome at things to come, what next
age hath in store. [*Ibid.*]

23. *Simon Steward's* ' coat of arms :'

French Charls would have these Coats to be thus
worn ;
When singly good, their better jointly born.
[*Ibid.*]

24. *Beestone Castle:* ' pictures' of—

When real walls are vanish'd quite
Painted ones doe us delight.

'Learned Leland is very confident that this castle shall see better times, deriving his intelligence from ancient predictions :'

Beestone in time its head aloft shall heave
If I, a prophet, prophets may believe.
                                        [Cambridgeshire.]

25.† *Daniel King:* 'on whom we will bestow this distick'
Cheshire to King and King to Cheshire owes
His light : each doth receive what each bestows.

'What is amiss in my poetry, shall be amended in my prayers for a blessing on his and all ingenious men's undertakings.'   [The Latin is]

Kingus Cestrensi, Censtrensis Patria Kingo
Lucem alternatim debet uterque suam.
                                        [Cheshire.]

26. *Dreams:* [Virgil: Aeneid vi. 893]

Dreames have two gates: one made [they say] of horn ;
By this port pass, true and prophetic dreames:
White ivory the other doth adorne ;
By this false shades and lying fancies streames.
                                        [Cornwall.]

27. *Tongilian:* 'I cannot take my leave of these tinners, untill I have observ'd a strange practice of them, that once in seven or eight years they burn down (and that to their great profit) their own melting houses.'

'I remember a merry epigram in Martial on one Tongilian who had his house in Rome causually (reputed) burnt, and gained ten times as much, by his friends' contribution to his loss :'

Gaining tenfold, tell truly, I desire
Tongilian, did'st not set thy house on fire.

[Cornish.]

[See the explanation in the sequel of the text. G.]

28. *Cornish:* 'They ever have been be-held men of valour. It seemeth in the reign of the aforesaid king Arthur they ever made up his van-guard, if I can rightly understand the barbarous verses of a Cornish poet :'

Brave Arthur, when he meant a field to fight
Us Cornish men did first of all invite:
Only to Cornish (count them Caesar's swords)
He the first blow in battle still affords. [*Ibid.*]

29. *Michael Blaunpayn:* 'It happened one Henry of Normandy, chief poet to our Henry the

Third, had traduced Cornwall, as an inconsiderable country, cast out by nature in contempt into a corner of the Land. Our Michael could not endure this affront : but full of poeticall fury, falls upon the libeller. Take a taste (little thereof will go far) of his strains :'

We need not number up her wealthy store
Wherewith this helpful land relieves her poor,
No sea so full of fish, of tinn no shore.

' Then as a valiant champion, he concludeth all with this exhortation to his countrymen :'
What should us fright if firmly we do stand ?
Bar fraud, then no force can us command.

' His pen so lushious in praising when so pleased, was as bitter in railing when disposed : witness this his satirical character of his aforesaid antagonist :'
Gamb'd like a goat, sparow-thigh'd, sides as boar,
    Hare-mouth'd, dog-nos'd, like mule thy teeth
    and chin :
Brow'd as old wife, bul-headed, black as more.
    If such without, then what are you within ?
By these my signs the wise will easily conster
    How little thou didst differ from a monster.
                                    [Cornish.]

30. *Richard Carew and Sir Philip Sidney in
'dispute extempore' at College:*

Ask you the end of this contest?
They neither had the better ; both the best.
[Cornish.]

31. *Sympathy:*

When thy neighbour's house doth burn
Take heed the next be not thy turn.
[Cumberland.]

32. *John Salkeld* 'presented to king James :
by whose arguments (and a benefice bestowed on
him in Somersetshire) he became a Protestant.
This he used in all companies to boast of "that
he was a royall convert." Nobisque dedit solatia
victor.'

And was it not a noble thing
Thus to be conquer'd by a king. [*Ibid.*]

[*Not* to be confounded with good John Salkeld
'ejected' in 1662 from Worlington, Suffolk.
See Calamy *s. n.* G.]

33. *Chatsworth:* [from Hobbes' De Mirabi-
libus Pecci].

Chatsworth, which in its bulk itself doth pride
And lord (both great) stands Derwens bank
   beside ;
Which slides still by the gate, as full of wonder
Through loud with stones above the house and
   under.   [Derbyshire.]

34. ‘ *Buxton Well:* [*Ibid.*]

Old men’s numb’d joynts new vigor here acquire ;
In frozen nerves this water kindleth fire.
Hither the creples halt, some help to find,
Run hence, their crutches unthank’t† left behind.
The barren wife here meets her husband’s love
With such success she strait doth mother prove.
                             [*Ibid.*]

† ‘ The Translator durst not be so bold as the
author.’

35. *Battle of Alcaser :*

A fatal fight, where in one day was slain
Three kings that were and one that would be fain.
                             [*Ibid.*]

36 *Sir Francis Drake:* ‘ This tetrastic made

on his corpse when cast out of the ship, wherein
he died, into the sea :’
Though Rome’s religion should in time return
   Drake, none thy body will ungrave again :

There is no fear posterity should burn
Those bones, which free from fire in sea remain.
[Devonshire.]

37. *Samuel Word:* ' Now because the pen of
a pupil may probably be suspected of partiality,
of an historian I will turn a translator and only
endeavour to English that character which one
[Dr Thomas Goad] who knew him as well as most
men and could judge of him as well as any man
doth bestow upon him.'

Go to, go on, deck (as thou doest) the chaire
With subtilty not light, slight, vague as air;
But such as Truth doth crown, and standing sure
Solidly fix'd will weighing well endure.
Antiquities' hid depths thou oft doest sound,
And School-men's whirl-pools which are so pro-
        found.
Distinction's threads none can so finely weave;
Or reason wrench, thy knowledge to deceive;
None thy quick sight, grave judgement, can beguile
So skill'd in tongues, so sinewy in style:
Add to all these that peaceful soul of thine
Meek, modest, which all brawlings doth decline.
[Durham.]

38. *Sir Henry Killigrew :* ' Now Katherine, his lady wrote these following verses to her sister Mildred Cecil, to improve her power with the Lord Treasurer her husband, that Sir Henry might be excused from that service [of ambassador to France]. We will endeavour to translate them, though I am afraid falling much short of their native elegance :'

If Mildred, by thy care, he be sent back whom I
    request,
A sister good thou art to me, yea better, yea, the
    best.
But if with stays thou keep'st him still or send'st
    where seas may part,
Then unto me a sister ill, yea worse, yea none
    thou art.
If go to Cornwall he shall please, I peace to thee
    foretell ;
But Cecil, if he set to seas, I war denounce.
    Farewell.   [Essex.]

39. † *Thomas Barington and ' Spouse'*—' See here a sympathizing wife, dying the next day after her husband, of whom it may be said'

He first deceased : she for few hours try'd
To live without him, lik'd it not, and dy'd.
                                        [*Ibid.*]

40. *Higre and Adria* [= Adriatic G.]—After quoting Drayton's description of the Higre, Fuller adds 'Had this been known to the Roman poet [Horace] when he thus envied against his shee-friend'

Thou art more light, more angry than
The cork, and uncouth Adrian.

'I say, had it been known, he would have changed Adria into Higrea, the former being a very calme in comparison of the latter.'—[Gloucestershire.] [I doubt good Fuller if thou speakest here from experience if I may judge from what the Adriatic has proved to me in sailing it over and over. G.]

41. *Thomas de la More:*

A man whose fame extended far
For arts in peace and feats in war.

[Gloucestershire.]

42. *Charles Butler:* author of a 'Book of Bees:'

Butler, he'l say (who these thy writing sees)
'Bees counsel thee or else thou counsel'st bees.

[Hampshire.]

43. *William, second son of King Edward the Third :* 'What I find written on the late monument of a noble infant may also serve for his epitaph.'

Living I could not speak, now dead I tel
Thy duty : think of death : and so farewell.
[Hertfordshire.]

44. *Alexander Nequam or Bad in English* : 'Many conceived themselves wondrous witty in making jests (which indeed made themselves) on his sirname.' .... 'Whereupon Nequam (to discompose such conceits for the future) altered the orthography of his name into Neckam. Another pass of wit there was . . . . . betwixt him and *Philip* Repington, bishop of Lincoln, the latter sending the challenge.'

Et *niger* et *nequam*, cum sis cognomine *Nequam;*
Nigrior esse potes, *nequior* esse *nequis.*
Both *black* and *bad*, whilst *Bad* tie name to thee
Blacker thou may'st but *worse* thou can'st not be.

To whom Nequam rejoyned :

Phi nota fœtoris, *lippus* malus omnibus horis :
Phi malus et *lippus*, totus malus ergo Philippus.

Stinks are branded with a *Phi; lippus* Latin for
blear-eye :
Phi and *lippus* bad as either ; then Philippus
worse together.

This [is his] epitaph :

> Wisdom's eclips'd, sky of the sun bereft
> Yet less the loss if like alive were left.
> A man discreet, in manners debonair
> Bad name, black face, but carriage good and
> fair. **[*Ibid.*]**

45.† *William of Ware :* ' He was instructor
to John Duns Scotus.'

And if the scholar to such height did reach
Then what was he who did this scholar teach ?
[*Ibid.*]

46. *Wye-salmon :*

> Salmon in Summer is not rare
> In Winter I of them do share.

for the river Wye affords brumal salmon, fat
and sound, when they are sick and spent in other
places.' **[Herefordshire]**

47. *Adam de Easton :* ' Pity it is so good a
scholar should have so barbarous an epitaph,
scarce worth our translation.'

N

Adam a famous father in arts all
He was a deep divine, *Cardi*-and-*nall*,
Whom England bred, St Cicelie hath given
His title—death at last gave heaven.

[Herefordshire.]

48. *William Sempster* :

Well I know these works he wrot
But for the time I know it not.   [*Ibid.*]

49. *Humphry Ely* :

Wonder not, reader, that with heresies
England is clouded : here her Sun he lies

[*Ibid.*]

50. *Rosamund :* 'buried in a little nunnery at
Godstowe nigh Oxford, with this epitaph.'

This tomb doth inclose, the world's fair rose, so
    sweet and full of savour
And smell she doth now, but you may guess how,
    none of the sweetest savour.   [*Ibid.*]
[See sequel in context.   G.]

51. *Sir Robert Cotton :*   ·

Camden to him, to him doth Selden, owe
Their glory : what they got from him did grow.

[Huntingdonshire.]

52. *Interpretation of a proverb :*

If thou know'st better, it to me impart
If not, use these of mine with all my heart.

[Kent.]

53. *Germans:*

'Mongst the old Teuch, lest one oretop his breed
To his sire's land doth every son succeed. [*Ibid.*]

54.† *Edmund, youngest son to Henry the Seventh* 'died before he was full five years of age.'
. . . 'Little notice generally is taken of this prince : and no wonder, for'

Who only act short parts in infant age
Are soon forgot they ere came on the stage.

[*Ibid.*]

55. *Sir James Hales:*

Seeing nought thou seest but faling in the best,
Mind thy own matters and leave God the rest.

[*Ibid.*]

56. *Richard Fletcher:* 'Queen Elizabeth knew full well'

The jewel vertue is more grac'd
When in a proper person cas'd. [*Ibid.*]

57. *Sir Thomas Wyat:*

Let Florence fair her Dante's justly boast
And royal Rome her Petrarch's numbered feet:
In English Wiat both of them doth coast
In whom all graceful eloquence doth meet.

[Kent.]

58. *New Kings:*

Subjects commonly do finde
New-made soveraigns most kinde.

[Lancashire.]

59. *Wills:* 'Richard Bancroft cancelled his
first will.' . .

He who never repented of doing ill
Repented that once he made a good Will.

[*Ibid.*]

60. *Worth:*

Nor will worth
Long be confin'd but make its own way forth.

[*Ibid.*]

61. *Fleet-hounds:* 'Such a *petronius* or fleet
hound, is two hounds in effect.

To the *petronian*, both the praise is due
Quickly to find and nimbly to pursue.

[Lincolnshire.]

62. *Grey-hounds :* ' Martial speaking of these greyhounds, thus expresseth himself :'

For's master, not himself, doth greyhound toil
Whose teeth to thee return the unhurt spoyl.'

[Lincolnshire.]

63. *Mastiffs :*

The British whelps no blemish know
But that they are not whelp'd for show.

[*Ibid.*]

64. *Lost* ' *commons :*' ' Long since Virgil said the same in effect of the men of Mantua, when they lost their lands to the souldiers of Augustus.'

See townsmen, what we by our jars are grown ;
And see for whom we have our tillage sown.

[*Ibid.*]

65. *Ayscough, bishop of Sarum :* murdered by Jack Cade :—

By people's fury mitre thus cast down
We pray henceforward, God preserve the crown.

[*Ibid.*]

66. *Thomas Goodrich :* ' It will [not] be amisse to insert and translate this distick made upon him :'

Both *good* and *rich*, well joyned, best rank'd
   indeed :
For *grace* goes first and next doth *wealth* succeed.
                                          [Lincolnshire.]

67. *Hampton Court :* [It] 'hath happiness
to continue in its former estate.'

I envy not its happy lot, but rather thereat
   wonder ;
There's such a rout, our Land throughout, of
   pallaces by plunder.   [Middlesex.]

68. *Fulke de Brent and his 'wife :'*
Now both of them be'ng brought into a bed
   By law and love and concord joynèd are ;
What law ? what love ? what concord did them
      wed ?
   Law lawless, loath'd love, concord which did
      jarr.   [*Ibid.*]

69. † *Katherine, 3d daughter of King Henry
the IIId :* 'She died in her very infancy, on
whom we will presume to bestow this epitaph :'
Wak't from the wombe, she on this world did
   peep
Dislikt it, clos'd her eyes, fell fast asleep.
                                          [London.]

70.† *Wives of Henry VIII:* ' Such as desire
to know the names, number and successe of all
six, may conceive King Henry thus speaking on
his death-bed :'

> Three Kates, two Nans, and one dear Jane I
> wedded ;
> One Spanish, one Dutch, and four English
> wives :
> From two I was divorc'd, two I beheaded,
> One died in child-bed, and one me survives.
> [*London.*]

71. *William Cotton, D.D.:* ' epitaph.'

> When th' queen from Paul to Peter did
> remove,
> Him God with Paul and Peter plac'd above.
> [*Ibid.*]

72. *Spenser:* ' epitaph :'

> Whilst thou did'st live, liv'd English poetry
> Which fears, now thou art dead, that she
> shall die. [*Ibid.*]

73. *London :*

> Potent in piety, in her people proud.
> [*Ibid.*]

74. *Charles II.:* 'a tetastric by Master Booth.'

Prince Charles, forgive me, that my silent
    quill
Joy'd not thy birth ; alas ! sore sick was I.
New hopes now come ; had I been silent still
I should deserve both to be sick and die.
                  [Westminster.]

75. *Bishop Aylmer:*

Eighteen years bishop and once banish'd
    hence
And twice a champion in the truth's defence.
                  [Norfolk.]

76. '*An end*': 'Virgil, I remember put a period to his Eclogue with'

    'We'll versifie no more
For do but hark, Hylax doth bark at th'
    entrance of the dore.'   [*Ibid.*]

77. *William Lilly:* 'This I will do for William Lilly (though often beaten for his sake) endeavour to translate his answer [to Skelton. G.]

With face so bold and teeth so sharp
Of viper's venome, why dost carp?
Why are my verses by thee weigh'd
In a false scale? May truth be said?
Whilst thou, to get the more esteem
A learnèd poet fain wouldst seem :
Skelton, thou art, let all men know it,
Neither learned nor a poet. [Norfolk].

78. *Sir Robert Dallington :* 'He was knighted
and preferred master of the Charter-house, where
the schoolmaster at his first entering, welcomed
him with a speech in Latine verse, spoken by a
schoolboy ; but sure he was more then a boy who
indited it.' . . . 'the last distick therein '—

Do not the least part of your trust disdain
Nor grudge of boys to take the care again.
[Northamptonshire.]

79. *John Fletcher :* 'It could [not] be laid
to Fletcher's charge, what Ajax doth to Ulysses'
[Ovid : Met. lib. 13].

When Diomede was gone
He could do nought alone.

For surviving his partner [Beaumont] he wrote
good comedies himself.' [*Ibid.*]

80. *Peter Pateshull:* would have been burned
save for his flight. 'This mindeth me of a passage of a frier who burned a book of Peter
Ramus, after the death of the author thereof;
and then and there used this distick in some
imitation of Ovid.

> Small book, thy fate I envy not,
>   (Without me) feel the flame;
> Oh had it been thy master's lot
>   He might have felt the same. [*Ibid.*]

81. *Laxton:*

> At Oundle born, what he did get
>   In London with great pain,
> Laxton to young and old hath set
>   A comfort to remain.   [*Ibid.*]

82. *Friars:*

Hear, why that they so much in England
    thriv'd:
When th' English earst in Palestine arriv'd,
The city Acon on the shore of Tyre
As next at hand, with arms did soon acquire

The captives, seeing so great wonders wrought,
There friers with them into England brought:
What was denied at home, they here anew

Churches and houses built.   In years but few
Increasing twig-like set by happy band
Or tree transplanted to a fruitful land.

[Northumberland.]

83. *Thomas Magnus:* ' He was an exposed
child'—' What the poet saith of the father of
Cadmus (commanding his son to find his lost
sister Europa or else never to return) that he was

Expressing in one act a mind
Which was both cruel and was kind

' Now it happened that some Yorkshire
clothiers coming in the dark (very early or late)
did light on this child, and resolved to pay both
for his nursing and education, the charge whereof
would not be great, equally divided betwixt them,
according to the proverb *Multorum manibus
grande levatur onus.'*

An heavy work is light to do
When many hands are put thereto.

[Nottinghamshire.]

84. *Venison*

Old wine did their thirst allay, fat venison
hunger.   [Oxfordshire.]

85. *Quarrels :*

Mark the Chronicles aright
When Oxford scholars fall to fight,
Before many months expir'd
England will with war be fir'd. [Oxfordshire].

86. † ' *Wife of Peter Martyr :* ' It happened
in the first of queen Elizabeth that the scholars
of Oxford took up the body of the wife of Peter
Martyr, who formerly had been disgracefully
buried in a dunghill, and interred it in the tomb
with the dust of St Frideswide.   Sanders addeth,
that they wrote this inscription (which he calleth
impium epitaphium) : Hic requiescit Religio cum
Superstitione : though the words being capable of
a favourable sense on his side, he need not have
been so angry.   However we will rub up our old
poetry and bestow another upon them.'

In tumulo fuerat Petri quæ Martyris uxor,
    Hic cum Frideswidâ virgine jure jacet
Virginis intactæ nihilum cum cedat honori,
    Conjugis in thalamo non temerata fides.
Si sacer Angligeniss cultus mutetur (at absit !)
    Ossa suum servent mutua tuta locum.
Intomb'd with Frideswide, deem'd a sainted maid
The wife of Peter Martyr here is laid :

And reason good, for women chaste in mind
The best of virgins come no whit behind.
Should Popery return (which God forefend !)
Their blended dust each other would defend.

[Oxfordshire.]

87. *War :*

Mars, Mars, bane of men, slaughter-stain'd spoiler
of houses. [Rutlandshire.]

88. *Sword :*

Sword which god Vulcan did for Daunus fixe
And quenched it when firy hot in Stix.

[Shropshire.]

89. *Ralph of Shrewsbury :* builder of a house
for the 'vicars-choral' of his cathedral : which in
an old picture is thus presented :

The Vicars' humble petition on their knees.
To us dispers'd i th' streets good father give
A place where we together all may live.
The gracious answer of the Bishop, sitting.
Your merits crave that what you crave be yielded ;
That so ye may remain, this place we've builded.

[*Ibid.*]

90. † *William Adams :* a great Benefactor. 'But
who for the present can hold from praising so
pious a performance ?'

Come, Momus, who delight do'st take
Where none are found, there faults to make :
And count'st that cost and care and pain
Not spent on thee, all spent in vain.
See this bright structure, till that smart
Blind thy blear-eyes and grieve thy heart.
Some cottage-schools are built so low
The Muses there must groveling go.
Here, whilst Apollo's harp doth sound,
The sisters nine may dance around ;
And architects may take from hence
The pattern of magnificence.
Then grieve not, Adams, in thy mind,
'Cause you have left no child behind :
Unbred ! unborn, is better rather,
If so, you are a second father
To all bred in this school so fair
And each of them thy son and heir. [Shropshire.]

91. *William Grocine:* on a ' pleasant maid . . .
in a love-frolic' pelting him with a snow-ball—

A snow-ball white at me did Julia throw ;
Who would suppose it? fire was in that snow.
Julia alone can quench my hot desire
But not with snow or ice, but equal fire
                                        [Bristol.]

92. *Staffordshire :* ' This county hath much

beauty in the very solitude thereof: witness Beau-
Desert or the Fair Wildernesse, being the beautiful
barony of the Lord Paget :'

And if their deserts here so rare devises
Pray then, how pleasant are their paradises.
[Staffordshire.]

93. *From Virgil :*

From Troy may the isle of Tenedos be spide
Much fam'd when Priam's kingdom was in pride,
Now but a bay where ships in danger ride
[*Ibid.*]

94. † *Cathedral-churches :*

And of the servants we so much commend
What was the mistress whom they did attend ?
[Suffolk.]

95. *Bury :*

Though furious fire the old town did consume
Stand this till all the world shall flaming fume
[*Ibid.*]

96. *St Edmund :*

As Denis by his death adorneth France :
Demetrius Greece : each credit to his place :
So Edmund's lustre doth our Land advance,
Who with his vertues doth his country grace.

Sceptre, crown, robe, his hand, head, corps
  renouns
More famous for his bonds, his bloud, his
  wounds.   [Suffolk.]

97. *Stephen Gardiner :* ' He is reported to have
died more than half a Protestant . . . . which
if so, then did he verifie the Greek and Latin
proverb,'

The *Gardiner* oft-times in due season
Spake what is true and solid reason. [*Ibid.*]

98. *Lydgate's* ' epitaph :'

Dead in this world, living above the skye
Intombed within this urn doth Lydgate lie
In former time fam'd for his poetry.
    All over England.   [*Ibid.*]

99. *Samuel Ward :* ' epitaph.'
Grant some of knowledge greater store
  More learnèd some in teaching ;
Yet few in life did lighten more
  None thundred more in preaching.

One of his sons, lately dead, was beneficed in
Essex : and following the counsel of the poet

What doth forbid but we may smile
And also tell the truth the while?

hath in a jesting way in some of his books, delivered much smart truth of the present times.

[Suffolk.]

100. *Sir Wm. Cordal :* ' epitaph.'

Here William Cordal doth in rest remain
Great by his birth, but greater by his brain.
Plying his studies hard, his youth throughout
Of causes he became a pleader stout.
His learning deep such eloquence did vent,
He was chose speaker of the Parliament.
Afterwards knight queen Mary did him make
And counsellor, State-work to undertake :
And Master of the Rolls. Well worn with age
Dying in Christ, heaven was his utmost stage.
Diet and clothes to poor he gave at large
And a fair Almshouse founded on his charge.

[*Ibid.*]

101. *Parkhurst to Jewel :*

Dear Jewel, scholar once thou wast to me
Now 'gainst thy will I scholar turn to thee.

[Surrey.]

O

102. *William Ockham* a 'contradicting spirit.'

But now he's dead, as plainly doth appear
Yet would denie it, were he living[1] here.

[Surrey.]

103. *Epigram :*

Neither with thee can I well
Nor without thee, can I dwell. [*Ibid.*]

104. *Dr Barlow :*

Barlow's wife, Agathe, doth here remain
Bishop, then exile, bishop then again.
So long she lived, so well his children sped
She saw five bishops her five daughters wed.

[Sussex.]

105. *Sir Thomas Shirley:*

Virtue and labour, learn from me thy father
As for success, child, learn from others rather.

[*Ibid.*]

106. *Heraldry-rhyme :*

The Bear he never can prevail
To Lion it for lack of tail.

[Warwickshire.]

107. *Baucis and Philemon : applied to Mr
and Mrs Underhill :*

But good old Baucis with Philemon, match'd
In youthfull years, now struck with equal age,

---

[1] And why not *if* 'living?' G.

Made poorness pleasant in their cottage thatch'd
And weight of want with patience did asswage.

[Warwickshire.]

. . . . . .

Because we liv'd and lov'd so long together
Let's not behold the funerals of either;
May one hour end us both! may I not see
This: my wife burried nor wife bury me

[*Ibid.*]

108 *Patrons:*

Let not Mæcenasses be scant
And Maroes we shall never want
For, Flaccus, then thy country-field
Shall unto thee a Virgil yield. [*Ibid.*]

109. *Custom:*

Beat Nature back, 'tis all in vain
With tines of fork 'twill come again.

[Westmoreland.]

110. *Queen Jane Seymour:* who died in child-
bed.

Soon as her Phœnix bud was blown
Root-Phœnix Jane did wither:
Sad, that no age a brace had shown
Of Phœnixes together. [Wiltshire.]

111. *Bonner:*

If one by shedding blood for bliss may hope
Heaven's widest gate for Bonner doth stand op'e
[Nemo] Nobody speaking to Bonner.
All call thee cruell and the spunge of blood :
But Bonner, I say, thou art mild and good.

[Worcestershire.]

112. *Geat:*

Geat, a stone and kind of gemm
In Lycia grows : but best of them
Most fruitfull Britain sends ; 'tis bright
And black and smooth and very light.
If rubb'd to heat, it easily draws
Unto itself both chaffe and straws.
Water makes it fiercely flame
Oyle doth quickly quench the same.

[Yorkshire.]

113. *Daphne:*

Into a bough her hair did spread
And from her armes two branches bred.

[*Ibid.*]

114. *Eustathius de Fauconbridge:*

All here are worthy, thou the worthiest ;
All fully wise, thou wiser than the rest.

[*Ibid.*]

115.† *Thomas Johnson:* 'Let us bestow this epitaph upon him'

Hic, Johnsone, jaces; sed, si mors cederet herbis.
Arte fugata tuâ, cederet illa tuis.
Here Johnson lies : could physick fence Death's
    dart
Sure Death had bin declinèd by his art.

[Yorkshire.]

116. *Robert the Scribe:* 'True of him.'

The tongue her task hath not yet done
When that the hand her race hath run.

[*Ibid.*]

117. *Rhyme:*

All lands do not bring
Nor all waters, every thing. [*Ibid.*]

118. *Cathedral of York:*

Of flowers that grow the flower's the rose ;
All houses so, this house out-goes.   [*Ibid.*]

119. *Albane Hill:*

The shoar resounded still
Nothing but *Hill* and *Hill.* [Wales.]

120. *Rhymes:*

> Verses justly do request
> Their writer's privacy and rest.

And

> 'Twas hard for any then to write
> And not a satyre to indite.   [Wales.]

121. *William Breton:*

Hard places which the Bible doth contain
I study to expound ; but all in vain
Without God's help, who darkness doth explain
And with his help nothing doth hard remain, etc.

122. *Wonders:*

> Wonders here by me are told
>   To many men well known ;
> But till my eyes shall them behold
>   Their truth I'll never own.

[Anglesea.]

123. *Richard Vaughan:*

Prelate of London (O immortal grace
Of thine own Britons) first who had that place.
He's good, who what men ought to do, doth
    teach ;
He's better, who doth do what men should preach.
You best of all, preaching what men should do
And what men ought to preach that doing too.

[Carnarvon.]

XV. Epitaph to the Memory of Denys Rolle Esq. in Bicton Church, Devonshire.[1]

The Remaines of
Denys Rolle
Esqvire.

His earthly part within this tomb doth rest
Who kept a covrt of honovr in his breast :
Birth, beavtie, witt and wisedom sat as peeres
Till Death mistooke his virtves for his yeares.
Or else Heaven envy'd Earth so rich a treasvre :
Wherein too fine the ware, too scant the measvre :
His movrnfvll wife her love to shew in part
This tomb bvilt here : a better in her heart
Sweete babe, his hopefvll heyre (Heaven grant
this boon)
Live bvt so well bvt oh dye not so soone.

Obijt. $\begin{cases} \text{Anno D'ne } 1638 \\ \text{Aetatis } 24. \end{cases}$

Reliqvit fili $\begin{cases} \text{vm. vnum} \\ \text{as : qvinqvac.} \end{cases}$

---

[1] See 'Danmonii Orientales Illustres or the Worthies of Devon etc. etc. By John Prince, Vicar of Berry-Pomeroy in the same Conntry, 1697 folio: p. 551. Of also Fuller's 'Worthies' (Devon)—In the former we read 'He [Dennis, Rolle Esq.] was buried in the parish church of Bickton aforesaid, about the 12th or 11th day of June A.D. 1638. In the which by the piety of his dearest lady was a noble

16. 'Andronicus.' [G. 4 verso-ed 1646.] [1]

' And now, let him alone to prevent their proceedings, by cutting both them and theirs off
(that no mindfull heire might succeed to their
spite) and that with all possible speed; for hee
steer'd his actions, by the compas of that character, which one made of him, as followeth.

I love at leasure, favours to bestow;
And tickle men by dropping kindnesse slow,
But my revenge, I in one instant spend,
That moment which begins [2] it, doth it end.

Half doing undoe's many, 'tis a sinne
Not to be soundly sinfull; to begin,
And tire; I'le do the work. They strike in vain,
Who strike so, that the stricken might complain.

---

monument, erected to his and her memory, of white marble,
where are seen lying at length his and her effigies lively and
curiously cut in alabaster, under a rich arch, adorned with
several coats of arms relating to the family. On a table of
black marble is found this inscription in letters of gold, made
by Dr Fuller.' The Rolle name continued and abides illustrious to the present generation. G.

[1] This I include among Fuller's, in deference to the sugges-
tion of Mr Wright, *as before.* Some others similarly introduced, I cannot recognise as his. G.

[2] *begings* in the original. G.

XVI. FIFTY-NINE
HITHERTO UNPUBLISHED EPIGRAMS.

NOTE.

As stated in our Introduction, Mr W. Carew Hazlitt sent a communication to Notes and Queries (3d Series, VII. pp. 352, 353) concerning a volume then in his possession, which contained contemporary MS. insertions. The 'Note' is as follows:—' In a copy of Crashaw's *Steps to the Temple*, with the Delights of the Muses, second edition 1648 8vo [it is a small 12°. G.] which fell in my way about three years ago, I discovered written upon the blank leaves,—as a portion of the copy was printed on one side only,—a large quantity of curious Manuscript matter, consisting partly of *excerpta* from printed works, but partly of original and inedited compositions. Among these, are upwards of fifty epigrams, chiefly upon religious subjects, by "Mr Thomas Fuller," and I forward herewith some account of the collection, which, as I have little or no doubt that "Mr Thomas Fuller" is identical with the Church-historian, cannot fail to be of interest to some of your readers.' [Here follows a selection of the headings of 42 of the Epigrams, and Mr Hazlitt adds, 'with about a dozen more:' which is within the mark. G.] 'In a different hand from the above are other epigrams, among which are several of an amatory cast. At the close of the volume occurs, with considerable appearance of having been written by the same person who has composed or transcribed the other pieces, the autograph of Dudley Lovelace, who has written his name a second time with an eye to a little *jeu de mots*, thus: Dudley Love-lasse, and this gentleman has apparently (for they are in the same hand or a very similar one) copied out portions of his brother's *Lucasta* upon some of the spare leaves, with here and there a variation from the printed edition. On the recto of p. 96 there are four verses from Lucasta with the signature of Richard Lovelace. The true history of the little book before me, might be curious and interesting, if it could be ascertained. There is surely ground for presuming that it has once been possessed by Dudley Posthumous Lovelace, the youngest brother of the ill-fated Cavalier Poet, Richard Lovelace, if not of the latter himself. I referred to the curiosity of the present copy of Crashaw in a note at p. 42, of my edition of the Poems of Richard Lovelace, 1864. 'W. Carew Hazlitt.'

In examining the volume I find on back of the engraved title-page and continued through other two pages, certain *memoranda* headed 'An Asylum for extremity,' and closed thus on reverse of 'the Table' (= Contents)

'finis of ye Asylum for

Laborious
love } extremity T. J. S.'

This portion is partly in short-hand characters, and differs, I think, from the Epigram hand-writing. Who was T. J. S. —if I correctly read the initials? Lovelace himself has a poem to Lady A[nne] L[ovelace] 'My asylum in a great extremity,' of which, *above* words seem an echo. Again: on the blanks from p. 75 to p. 77, there are 18 numbered 'Epigrams' which would seem to belong to Crashaw, though not assigned to him. Fuller's 'Epigrams' fill the blanks from p. 78 to 84. I adhere with literal fidelity to the manuscript—placing in brackets my filling up of less plain contractions—and I have to acknowledge the admirable help and rare insight of W. Aldis Wright, Esq., M.A., Trinity College, Cambridge, in deciphering the somewhat intricate and difficult hand-writing and meaning. The figures 1, 2, etc., point to a few slight explanatory Notes appended. Under Epigrams 10, 40, 53 are references to 'Pisgah-Sight' which confirm their Fullerian authority. These might be multiplied. But specially note Epigram 33: and as bearing the true mint-mark Nos. 2, 4, 6, 7, 10, 12, 13, 18, 19, 21, 22, 24, 27, 31, 34, 35, 40, 42, 43, 44, 45, 47, 54, 55, 58, 59. G.

XVI. "EPIGRAMS BY THO: FULLER."

1. On Adam.[1]

When modest—sinful, w[he]n cloath'[d]—nak'd
    in minde,
Wⁿ knoweinge—ignorant: wⁿ seeinge—
    blinde (1).

2. On Noah.   A ridle.

No: wares he caried w[hi]ch he m[ean]t to sel
    Of pirats ferrelesse: for no harbor bound
All winde tho turninge served his turn as wel
    He only wisht for to be run on ground. (2).

3. On Leah:

Too tender were her eeys; if God so please
    Would al mens harts were 'sicke of her
    disease. (3).

---

[1] Cf. the quotation from 'Hainous Sinne' etc. in our Introduction page 13 [III. st. 6], almost identical.   G.

4. On Joseph & his M^rs (4).

He might have been oc'rcome by makeinge stay
Who overcame by runninge quite away
When Josep[h] to his m^rs would not yeild
Sure then he overcame in Loosecoat [1] field.

5. On Ziporah circum : her sons. (5).

Sheddinge her sons blood sav'd her husband's life.
But then her tongue cuts sharper then a knife :
With her sons fore-skine so she thought to fit him
Thrown at his feet she in ye teeth did hit him.

6. On Moses Smiteinge ye Rocke. (6).

He formerly complain'd, my tongue's too slowe
But surely then his tongue to[o] fast did goe.

7. On the Batle with Amelacke. (7).

The wind i' th' victory, where did it stand [?]
Looke on ye weathercocke on Moses' hand :
His hand's no weathercocke I cal to minde
Yt's turnèd about, but this doth turn ye winde.

---

[1] A place near Stamford w[h]ere a Batle in Edw: 4 time
[The preceding note is in the Manuscript. Mr Wright as
before, has been good enough to send me the following
' *Loosecoat-field* is mentioned by Speed as the scene of a
battle fought near Stamford in the reign of Edward the
Fourth—so called because the defeated party in the hurry
of their flight threw away their coats—Speed, History of
Great Britain p. 680 edi. 1611.' G.]

8. On Joshauah. (8).

Weake faith y^t one days station doth comand
Brave Keplar (9) make ye sun for ever stand.

9. On ye Alter Ed. (10).

This Alter they did piously Intend
Pray God none ere be bu[i]lt to worser end.

10. Sampson's Jawe bone. (11).

Water [1] from Horse-hoofe : [2] 'tis a fable thinge
'Tis now an Asses Jawe did yei[l]d a Springe. [2]

11. On Ephraimites fals pronunc: Shiboleth (12).

They wanted H in their pronnunciation
Sure H : was then a heavy aspiration :
Schin was their theta & much blood it spils
To them ye word was true, ye letter kils.

12. On Elijah taken vp into heaven (13).

He'es Israel's chariot : who y^o like espi'de
To see a chariot in a chariot ride.

---

[1] Helicon. F.   [2] Pegasus. F.
[3] In 'Pisgah-Sight' p. 229, we read ' 'tis true an Asses
Jawe did yei[l]d a Springe ' p. 229, ed. 1650. G.

13. On Zachens (14).

Hee climb'd A fig-tree : this I dare ad more (15)
No barren fig-tree then : good frute it bore

14. On ye Powder plot (16).

The plot was onely in Intention wrought
Y^e plotters were to execution brought.

15. On Vaine Excuses.

When men do sin themselves they blame ye divel
Y^o divel doth their sin : they do ye evil.

16. On Gallants cloakes.

Without plaine cloath, within plush : but I doubt
Y^o wearer's worst within & best without.

17. On Popish Interpretation of Scripture.

Christ : Drinke al of this at ye comunion table
Pope : By al, ye clergy, their are only meant
Paul : Mariage Amongst al men 's honorable
Pope : All, there's ye Laity y^{ts} paul's intent.
Christ : Is't so indeed : w^t X[t], saith or St Paul
yts nothinge : w^t ye pope saith, all in all.

18. On Sin.

We paint ye divel blacke : us to requite
The blackamore's do paint ye divel white :

Thus juglers count spendinge yᵉ only (17)
vice
And spenders make it to be avarice
And every man whereof himselfe is free
Yᵗ he conceives yᵉ only sin to be.

19. Whether Scripture or tradition [is] yᵉ
mother of faith.

Scr. Yᵉ child is mine, of certaine Sᵗ I
bare it

Trad: Sᵗ, it's mine & I must therefore
share it :

Solomon: Yᵗ then this matter better be decided
Bringe forth a sword & let it be
divided (18).

Trad: O wel sᵈ Sᵗ yᵉ Judgmᵗ is wel spent
Let it be hers & mine Indifferent.

Scrip: O no not so, alive for pity save it
Let me have't al or let her wholy
have it.

Solomon: O now I see this woman is yᵉ
mother
Give her yᵉ child and pack away yᵉ
other.

20. On Pope Innocent.

Pope Innocent cheife of yᵉ Roman Rout
Answers his name : but how if In : were out.

P

21. On Corn hoarders.[1]

Why do'st y^u (19) hoard up corn for mice w^n
faine
Y^e people would it buy : oh knave in graine.

22. On Joseph's M^{rs} (20).

Bec : chast-minded Joseph did deny
To ly with her, she wretch on him did ly.

23. On Jacob (21).

Cheape rate he gave & always thinkes to gett
For birthright, pottage : fore ye bless^g
meat.

24. On Paul's Jorney to Damascus (22).

Blest blindnes wch did ope his ghostly eyes
And fal y^t made him into heaven rise.

25. On ye Philistins (23).

Sampson's firebranded foxes vext them sore
Our Fox (24) his firebrand vext ye papists
more.

---

[1] Fuller would have agreed with like-minded Dr William
Smith in his memorable ' Blacksmith' sermon, wherein he
paraphrases St Basil 'in one of those sermons that he
wrought against the covetous cormorants or corn-morants
of his time' ['The Blacksmith' 1606.] G.

26. On Michal's mockeinge (25).

W[ha]t Issue came there of a deed so bad
Alas ! no issue : child she never had.

27. On Peter's words 'shal I smite?' (26).

He gave no care to hear w[ha]t Christ would
   say
But presently tooke Malchus' care away.

28. On Bugbears.

Scare not thy children w[it]h false and foolish
   fears
But rather tel them of Elisha's beares (27).

29. On Sampson.

Porter, who Gaza's (28) gates op'd without
   stay
Porter who on his backe bore gates away.

30. On Manasse (29).

W[he]n far from home this Cap[ti]f longe was
   sent
Home came he to himselfe & did repent.

31. On Jacob (30).

W[he]n to his thigh ye Lord a touch did send
Jacob did halt before his dearest frend.

32. On Noah's dove (31).

The newes she brought by mouth tho nothing spake
Whose nothinge answer did in folio make.

33. A prayer.

My soul is stainèd w[i]th a dusky colour
Let thy Sonne be y° sope I'le be y° Fuller (32).

34. On Peter's Sinkeinge (33).

Cephas : w[ha]ts yᵃ (?) a stone : yea so I thinke
A heavey stone : for it began to sinke.

35. On his Successors.

If in y° sea y° popes durst him succeed
Where he was duckt, they would be drown'd
indeed.

36. On pride in cloaths.

Eagles have none but peacockes have brave traine
Subjects goe fine in cloaths, y° kinge goes plaine.

37. On Zacheus.

So I be good I care not to be tall
I'de rather be Zacheus then A Saul (34).

38. On Musculus (35).

This preacher turn'd A weaver forc't by need
How many weavers preachers do proceed.

39. One more knave then foole.

Nabal's a foole : read backeward & you have
His nature truly, Laban, yts a knave (36)

40. On David's three Worthy's (37).

Wast not stronge water w[hic]h 3 men so mighty
Ventur'd their lives for : yes, 'twas Aqua
vitæ. [1]

41. On Sampson (38).

Where lay ye strength of Sampson? even there
Where Gallants pride now lys : in their longe
hair.

42. A prayer.

Hard is my heart, Lord, to my greife I feele
Be y^u ye Loadstone, it shal be ye steele.

43. On ye Men of Sodom (39).

Most bad is in A Lottery : good but one
And ye good lot God drewe from thence alone.

---

[1] Cf. 'Pisgah-Sight' as before p. 299 on Aqua Vitæ. This
peculiar wording is also found in the ' Divine Poems' of
Thomas Washbourne D.D. (1654), e.g. of penitent tears.

' That *Aqua vitæ* Thou dost prize (page 14).
And at page 41—

' Th' *Aqua vitæ* which from Christ's side came.' G.

44. On Naboth accused (40.)

W[ha]t ground of such false crimes in hi[m] was
   found
Alas, his vineyeard y.^t was All ye ground.

45. On Jacob.

Stout souldier[1] who's yet[2] vnborn did fight (41).
   Great conqueror who queld ye lord of might.

46. On Ehud (42).

Who so wel set himselfe to understand
   May see God's finger plaine in Ehud's hand.

47. On ye Israelites in ye Wildernes.

Their sutes did hold til 40 yeares were past (43)
   Sure in our lawe some Sutes as longe do
   last.

48. On Perseverance.

Joash relaps'd, Manasse did Amend
   Begin with Joash, with Manasse end (44).

49. On James & John wishinge fire on ye Samaritans (45).

The sons of thunder was enough for you
   You need not to be sons of Lightning too.

---

[1] A trisyllable. G.   [2] Who as yet. G.

50. On Paul's danger (46).

Shipwracke escap't, no sooner come to land
But straight another danger is at hand:
Him men a murderer count, a wondrous thing
To bite him whom ye serpent would not
sting.

51. On Jael (47).

When Sisera sure as A naile was dead
Then Jael truly hit ye naile o'th' head:
He never dream't of her, she boldly say (48)
But yet she tooke hi[m] napking [napping] as he
lay.

52. On Hezekiah (49).

The sun In goeinge backe w[ha]t did it showe
Y^t Hezekiah's life should forward goe
A fig to hi[m] restor'd his life Againe:
How many popes have since by figs been slaine

53. On Jehosophat (50).

W[he]n he with wicked Ahab tooke A part
He sd to hi[m] I'me never [1] as y^u art
But w[it]h ye Aramites wel match't was he
Who timely tooke hi[m] Ahab for to me.

---

[1] Query—a mistake for 'I'm ever' or I'm even. See
1 Kings xxii 4; 'Pisgah-Sight' as before, p. 83. G.

54. On Isaace (51).

Whilst patient Isaace, at ye Alter lyes
Y^e Lord himselfe Alter'd ye Sacrifice :
A willinge minde of God is not despis'd
Isaacke was offer'd but not sacryfic'd.

55. On Sampson's weapons (52).

The silliest creature we do count ye Asse
Y^e fox doth always for ye wisest passe :
With Asse's Jawes Sampson his foes doth quaile
& flaps he gave them w[it]h a foxes taile.

56. On Japthaes daughter (53).

He kil'd her not say some but only stay'd
Her fro[m] ill marryinge : oh y^t kills a maide.

57. On Ely ye priest (54).

The newes of th' Ark's captivity once spoken
His hart was broke before his necke was broken
No wonder Ely was so tender harted
Y^e priest must needs dy w[he]n ye Ark's
      dep'[ar]ted.

58. On Sampson & John Baptist (55).

Much do I muse w[he]n I on Sampson thinke
So stronge, whose mother tasted no stronge drink
But yet John Baptist is A wonder rather
A cryer's voice, begot of A dumb father.

59. On Christ Lookinge on Peter (56).

Tho Peter w[it]h his tongue did Christ deny
Yet Christ, he ownèd Peter with his eye:
Peter who was with night of feares ore-drawn
But w[he]n ye Cocke did crowe ye day did dawn.

NOTES.

1. Adam: Cf. Genesis c. iii. vv. 7, 8.
2. Noah: Cf. Genesis c. vii.
3. Leah: Cf. Genesis c. xxix. 17.
4. Joseph: Cf. Genesis c. xxxix.
5. Zipporah: Cf. Exodus c. iv. 24-26.
6. Moses: Cf. Exodus c. iv. 10, with Numbers c. xx. 10
and Ps. cvi. 33.
7. Amelacke: Cf. Exodus c. xvii. 8-16.
8. Joshua: Spelled as *ante*, though I am not sure that the
first '*a*' was not intended to be blotted out. In the
MS. it is blackened. Cf. Joshua c. x. 12. y^t = that.
9. Keplar: The great astronomer 'Kepler' who so advanced
astronomical discovery. Query—mako = for makes
or made?
10. Ed: Cf. Joshua xxii. 34.
11. Sampson: Cf. Jugdes c. xv. 16.
12. Shiboleth: Cf. Judges c. xii. 6.
13. Elijah: Cf. 2 Kings c. ii. 12.
14. Zacheus: Zacchæus: Luke c. xix. 1-10.
15. Ad more admire, with a play on the words '*add more.*
16. Powder-Plot: so long celebrated in '5th November'
anniversary Sermons and Prayers.
17. 'Greatest,' is here written above the line.
18. 'Divided:' Cf. 1 Kings c. iii. 25 *seqq*.
19. 'Yu' the Latin 'tu,' thou: repeated in the MS.

20. Joseph: Cf. Note 4 *supra*.   The 'Bee' is probably a contraction for 'because.'

21. Jacob: Cf. Genesis c. xxv. 29–34 and c. xxvii. 19 *seqq.*

22. Paul: Cf. Acts c. ix. 3–9.

23. Philistines: Cf. Judges c. xv. 4.

24. Fox = John Foxe the Martyrologist.

25. Michal: Cf. 2 Samuel c. vi. 16 and 20–23.

26. Peter: Cf. St John c. xviii. 10: and the parallel passages.

27. Elishas bears: Cf. 2 Kings ii. 24.

28. Gaza in MS. is spelled 'Gara'—Cf. Judges c. xvi. 1–3.

29. Manasse = Manasseh — Cf. 2 Chronicles c. xxxiii. 1–20.

30. Jacob: Cf Genesis c. xxxii. 25, 31, 32.

31. Noah's dove: Cf. Genesis c. viii. 8, 9.

32. A prayer: Perhaps this pun-wit even in prayer is as self-authenticating a characteristic as is to be found in these Epigrams. Our Worthy delighted to play on his own name e.g. in his own epitaph 'Here lies Fuller's earth.'

33. Cephas: Cf. St John c. i. 42, with St Matthew c. xiv. 30.

34. Zacheus: Cf. *supra* note 14.

35. Musculus: a Memoir of this Reformer and Scholar is given in 'Abel Redevivus.'

36. Nabal: Cf. 1 Samuel c. xxv. 3, 25.

37. David's three Worthies: Cf. 2 Samuel c. xxiii. 9.

38. Sampson's hair: Cf. Judges c. xvi. 17 *seqq.*

39. Sodom: Cf. Genesis xix. 15 *seqq.*

40. Naboth: Cf. 1 Kings c. xxi. 1 *seqq.*

41. Jacob: Cf. Genesis c. xxv. 22.

42. Ehud: Cf. Judges iii. 15 *seqq.*

43. Israel in the Wilderness: Cf. Deuteronomy c. xxix. 5.

44. Perseverance: Cf. Note 29 *supra:* and Judges vi. 31 *et alibi.*

45. James and John: Cf. St Luke ix. 24, with St Mark c. iii. 17.

46. Paul's danger: Cf. Acts c. xxviii. 3 *seqq.*
47. Jael: Cf. Judges iv. 21, 22. and v. 26.
48. Query—gay?
49. Hezekiah: Cf. 2 Kings xx. 7, 11: and parallels in Isaiah.
50. Jehosophiat = Jehoshaphat. Cf. 2 Chronicles c. xviii. and 2 Chronicles xviii. 31 and xix. 2.
51. Isaac: Cf. Genesis c. xxii. 12.
52. Sampson: Cf. *supra* 11 and 38.
53. Jeptha's daughter: Cf. Judges c. xi. 30 *seqq.*
54. Ely the priest: Cf. 1 Samuel c. iv. 18.
55. Sampson and John the Baptist: Cf. Judges xiii. 5 with St Luke i. 20.

G.

APPENDIX.

---◆◇◆---

FULLER'S FORM OF PRAYER.

S stated in our Introduction there follows here the ' Form' which our Worthy was wont to use in his extra-Prayer-Book ' devotions.'

Concerning it, the rare anonymous ' Life' (1662) observes, ' A constant form of prayer he used as in his family so in his publique ministry ; onely varying or adding upon speciall occasions or occurences intervening required, because not only hesitation (which the good Doctor for all his strength of memory and invention, was afraid of before so awful a presence as the majesty of heaven) was in prayer more offensive than other discourse ; but because such excursions in that duty, in the extempore way, was become the idol of the multitude' (p. 81). The ' Form' itself is preserved in the exceedingly scarce volume whose title-page I now give.

PULPIT SPARKS

OR CHOICE

FORMS

OF

PRAYER,

BY SEVERAL

REVEREND and GODLY
DIVINES
USED by them, both before
and after SERMON.
WITH other PRAYERS, for
extraordinary occasions,

TOGETHER,

WITH Dr HEWYTTS,
last PRAYER,

BY,

Dr Reeve.	*M. Ball.*
Dr Gillingham.	*M. Goddard.*
Dr Jer. Taylor.	*M. Nat. Hardy.*
Dr Hewytt.	*M. Hull.*
Dr Wilde.	*M. Jo. Marston.*
Dr Griffith.	*M. Mackerness.*
Mr Tho. Fuller.	*M. Sparks.*

London, *Printed for* W. Gilbert-
son *at the Bible in* Giltspur-
street, 1659.

The date is 1659 though Mr Russell ['Memorials of Fuller'] gives it as 1658. The preface 'To the judicious, and religious reader' is signed '*Tho. Reeve*'—query author of that vivid and remarkable folio, 'The Plea of Niniveh' and various memorable Sermons.'

The volume is a very small 12mo. and Fuller's Prayer occupies pp. 156–171. G.

MR T. F. HIS

EVENING PRAYER.

ET the Words of my mouth, and the thoughts of all our hearts be now and ever acceptable in thy sight, O Lord our strength and our Redeemer.

O Eternal Lord God, infinite in thy greatnesse, incomprehensible in thy glory, whose pure and just Eyes cannot behold either sin or sinners with the least look of approbation; be not offended with thy servants; it will be little comfort for us in these glorious attributes; we come to them that may tender most consolation to us: Oh Lord God, who in Christ Jesus art a mercifull and a reconciled Father to all such sinners as sincerely from their Souls desire and endeavour to repent and believe; thy providence hath brought us unto this place to offer unto thy Majesty our evening sacrifice of prayer and thanksgiving, and to be made partakers of a portion of thy most holy Word; truly Lord we have just cause

to fear lest our prayers, instead of that blessing
we now desire, draw down that curse which they
deserve upon us; we have inflamed the corruptions of our natures with the manifold rebellions
of our lives, which have been nothing else but
one constant breach of thy ten commandements;
true Lord, the law in our minds, our spirit, our
new creature, our regenerate half, our light, clearly
knows and chearfully acknowledges all and every
one of thy commandements for pure, and just,
and holy; but the law in our members, our
darknesse, our flesh, our old Creature breaks
them daily in thought, word, and deed; we all
of us have been foul and flat Idolaters, erecting
the Idols of our own profit and pleasure in the
Chapels and Closets of our hearts, and then and
there have fallen down upon the bended knees of
our Souls, and worshipt them, by regarding our
lust more than the fulfilling of thy will in thy
word; that sacred name of thine whereby we
hope to be saved, we have taken in vain; we have
done that on thy day, the Lord's day, which we
can justifie or avouch on no day; we have not
given that reverence and respect to our Superiors
placed over us which thou requirest at our
hands; we have broken all the commandements
of the second Table in our demeanour towards
our neighbours, and in our deportment to our

own Souls and bodies ; and here Lord we are ashamed to confesse the manifold circumstances of our sins in the presence and hearing of man, who, vile, bold wretches were no whit ashamed or afraid to commit them when we knew full well that the high God of Heaven and Earth did at that instant behold us ; now lend us of thy Spirit effectually to admire at thy patience and longsuffering towards us, who permits such prophane and presumptuous sinners at this hour of our lives still to remain from Hell fire ; surely Lord there are many in that pit of perdition, whose sins against thee were never aggravated with those high circumstances ; O Lord, we have no variety of reasons to move thee to mercy, we have no exchange of motives to perswade thee to pitty, but only the same over and over again, for thy own sake, for thy names sake, for thy mercies sake, for thy Son and our Saviour Christ Jesus his sake forgive our sins, for they are great ; wash the guilt & filth of our sins away in his blood ; and Lord for the time to come give us grace to spend the remainder of our dayes in our several Callings to thy glory ; Lord grant that we may not only labour to have our sins pardoned to us, but also strive to have so much favour with thee, that before our deaths we may have our sins forgive-

ness assured ; for our comfort, grant Lord that
we may betake our selves to do the one thing
necessary ; let us not have our oyl to buy when
we should have it to burn ; teach us O Lord that
sicknesse is a time not to do but to suffer ; and
gracious Lord grant that our work being done,
and the books crost in the times of our healths,
we may be comforted when we come to dye, and
to resign our Souls into the hands of a faithfull
Creator and gracious redeemer. Blesse us with
thy whole Church scattered far and wide over
the face of the whole Earth ; Lord, what particulars to pray for, we know not, we dare not,
we humbly tender a blank into the hands of an
almighty God; write therein Lord what thou
wilt, when thou wilt, where thou wilt, by whom
thou wilt, only in thine own time work out
thine own honour and glory ; in the mean time
give us faith to believe it, patience to expect,
diligence to observe, and zeal to pray fervently
for it ; to this end blesse all those whom thine
own self in lawfull authority hast placed over
us, by what name or title soever known unto
us ; blesse their counsels and consultations, and
make them under thy self the happy instru-
ments of the good of this Nation. Be present
with us and President amongst us, at this time
in the hearing and handling of thy holy Word ;

Lord let not the manifold corruptions and the more imperfections of thy servant hinder the operation of thy word, but give me to speak it plainly to every capacity, methodically to every member, effectually to every conscience that shall be here present, so that it may sink in all our hearts, and bring forth fruit in the amendment of our lives and conversations. This, and what else thy wisdome sees fitter for us than we can aske or desire, we beg at thy hands in the name and mediation of Jesus Christ. *Our Father, etc.*

Crawford & M'Cabe, Printers, 7 George Street, Edinburgh.

Books by the

REV. ALEXANDER B. GROSART,

Prince's Road United Presbyterian Church, Liverpool.

I. ORIGINAL.

1. Small Sins. 3d edn., with additions, royal 16mo, cloth antique, price 1s. 6d., pp. 119.

2. Jesus Mighty to Save : or Christ for all the World and all the World for Christ. 3d edn., with additions, royal 16mo, cloth antique, pp. 204, price 2s.

3. The Prince of Light and the Prince of Darkness in Conflict : or the Temptation of Jesus. Newly Translated, Explained, Illustrated and Applied. Crown 8vo, pp. xxxiv. and 360, price 5s. [New and much enlarged Edition in preparation.]

4. The Lambs All Safe : or the Salvation of Children. 3d ed., with considerable additions, 18mo, cloth antique, price 1s.

5. Drowned : a Sermon in Memorial of the Death by drowning in Lochleven of Mr John Douglas. 3d edn. (3000) cr. 8vo, price 4d.

6. The Blind Beggar by the Wayside : or Faith, Assurance and Hope. 32mo, 4th edn., price 1½d. For enclosure in letters.

⁎ ⁎ Translated into Efik by William Anderson, Old Calabar, W. Africa. 12°.

7. Joining the Church : or Materials for Conversations between a Minister and intending Communicants. 18mo, cloth antique, price 1s., 2d edn.

8. The Helper of Joy, 2d edn., 18mo, cloth antique, price 1s.

9. Recollections of Prayer-Meeting Addresses on Some of the Questions and Prayers of the Bible.

10. Thoroughness.

11. Tears or Consolation for 'The Poor in Spirit.'

12. Sundays at. Sea : or What God says of the Sea and Sailors. [Nos. 9 to 12 in preparation].

13. Memoir of Richard Sibbes, D.D. 8vo (*See below*).

14. Memoir of Thomas Brooks, author of 'Precious Remedies,' etc. etc. 8vo (*See below*).

15. Memoir of Herbert Palmer, B.D. 8vo (*See below*).

16. Memoir of Henry Airay, D.D. (prefixed to reprint of his Commentary on Philippians). 4to.

17. Memoir of Thomas Cartwright, B.D. (prefixed to reprint of his Commentary on Colossians). 4to.

18. Memoir of John King, D.D., Bishop of London (prefixed to reprint of his Commentary on Jonah). 4to.

19. Memoir of John Rainolds, D.D. (prefixed to reprint of his Commentaries on Obadiah and Haggai). 4to.

20. Memoir of Richard Stock (prefixed to reprint of his Commentary on Malachi). 4to.

21. Memoir of Samuel Torshell (prefixed to reprint of his Exercitation on Malachi). 4to.

22. Memoir of Richard Bernard, B.D. (prefixed to his Exposition of Ruth). 4to.

23. Memoir of Thomas Pierson (prefixed to reprint of his Exposition of 'Select Psalms'). 4to.

---

24. Memoir of Samuel Smith (prefixed to reprint of his 'David's Blessed Man'). 4to.

25. Memoir of Richard Gilpin, M.D. (prefixed to reprint of his 'Demonologia Sacra'). 8vo.

*** 100 large paper copies, with Portrait and fac-simile, price 15s. 6d.

26. Memoir of Michael Bruce (*See below*) author of 'Ode to Cuckoo,' 'Hymns,' etc.

27. Hymns. (*For private circulation*). Royal 32mo.

II. EDITED.

28. The Works, with Memoir, Introduction and Notes, of Richard Sibbes, D.D., Master of Katherine Hall, Cambridge, and Preacher of Gray's Inn, London. 7 vols. 8vo, £1, 11s. 6d.

29. The Works, with Memoir and Notes, of Thomas Brooks, 6 vols. 8vo, 25s.

30. The Works of Michael Bruce, with Memoir, Introduction and Notes. Cr. 8vo, 3s. 6d.

*** Large paper edition, with numerous original Photographs, 10s. 6d.

31. The Works—with Memoir, Essay and Notes—of Robert Fergusson precursor of Burns. Cr. 8vo, 3s. 6d. (Portrait and Illustrations.)

32. Lord Bacon not the Author of 'The Christian Paradoxes.' Being a Reprint of 'Memorials of Godliness,' by Herbert Palmer, B.D.; with Introduction, Memoir, Notes and Appendix. Large paper, with Portrait, 8vo, 10s. 6d. 100 copies only : Small paper cr. 8vo, 3s 6d.: 150 *copies only.*

33. Selections from the Unpublished Writings of Jonathan Edwards, of America : with Introduction and Fac-similes. Royal 8vo, 7s. 6d. (300 copies only.)

34. The Grand Question Resolved—What must we do to be saved? Instructions for a Holy Life : by the late Reverend Divine Mr Richard Baxter. Recommended to the Bookseller a few days before his death, to be immediately printed for the good of souls. 1692.

₊ *Unknown to Biographers and Bibliographers,* cr. 8vo. [*See next*].

35. Annotated List of the Writings of Richard Baxter, author of The Saint's Everlasting Rest : made from Copies of the Books and Tractates themselves. Cr. 8vo. With No. 34, 3s. 6d : thick paper 5s.

36. The Poems and Translations in Verse (including Fifty-nine hitherto unpublished Epigrams, etc.) of Thomas Fuller, D.D., for the first time collected and edited, with Introduction and Notes. Cr. 8vo., 5s. 6d. : large paper (100 copies only) 10s. 6d.

₊ One of the 'Divine Poems' herein reprinted fetches in the book-market from £5, 5s. to £10, 10s., *i.e.* 'David's Hainous Sinne, Heartie Repentance, Heavie Punishment: another, the 'Pancgyrick' on Charles II. from £2, 2s. to £3, 3s. Besides these there are all his Verses and Translations from his numerous prose Works, hitherto unpublished Epigrams, etc. etc. Printed for Private Circulation : *a limited edition.*

₊ Other privately printed Works of old Worthies, in *immediate preparation.*

London : J. NISBET & CO. HAMILTON, ADAMS, & CO.

Edinburgh : WILLIAM OLIPHANT & CO.

Liverpool : ARCHIBALD FERGUSON, Bold Street.